WHAT MAKES RICH

Money Mindset on Planning, Budgeting, Saving, and Investing to Gain Financial Freedom

Tim Wealth

Copyright 2024 Tim Wealth

All rights reserved. No part of this book may be reproduced or transmitted in any form or by any means, electronic, or mechanical, including photocopying, recording, or by any information storage and retrieval systems, without written permission from the author, except by a reviewer who may summarize brief passages in a review.

Disclaimer

This book is intended to provide our readers with information and motivation. It is sold with the knowledge that the publisher is not engaged to provide any form of psychological, legal, or other professional advice. Each page's content is the sole expression and opinion of the author. Neither the publisher nor the individual author(s) shall be responsible for any physical, psychological, emotional, financial, or commercial damages, including but not limited to special, incidental, consequential, or other damages. Our points of view and rights are the same: you are solely accountable for your decisions, actions, and outcomes.

About The Author

Tim Wealth is a renowned figure in business, finance, and personal growth. With a long and impressive career, Tim has honed his expertise to become a trusted source of knowledge and inspiration for those seeking financial mastery and entrepreneurial success.

As a highly respected coach, Tim has mentored numerous individuals on the intricacies of personal finance, expanding their businesses, and finding lucrative money-making opportunities. His unique combination of practical wisdom and motivational skills has propelled his clients to new levels of financial abundance and professional accomplishment.

Tim's written works are pillars of guidance for those navigating the complexities of wealth management. Through his acclaimed books, he shares profound insights on savings, budgeting, financial planning, and retirement security, providing readers with a roadmap to lasting financial prosperity.

Beyond his role as an author and coach, Tim is a catalyst for transformation, igniting ambition and possibility in the hearts of his audience. His dynamic speaking engagements and workshops inspire individuals, businesses, and organizations to pursue their dreams with unwavering determination and strategic clarity.

With a steadfast commitment to empowering others and a proven track record of success, Tim Wealth continues to impact the landscape of personal finance and entrepreneurial achievement. He guides generations toward a future filled with unlimited opportunities and financial fulfillment.

See What People Are Saying About This Book

"Tim Wealth's 'What Makes Rich' is a game changer!" As someone who has always wanted financial freedom but didn't know where to begin, this book gave me the guidance I needed. Tim simplifies complex financial topics, from sensible budgeting and saving suggestions to effective investing techniques. If you want to gain control of your finances and generate wealth for the future, don't wait to get a copy!"

Sarah Johnson, Entrepreneur.

"I cannot recommend 'What Makes Rich' enough! Tim Wealth doesn't just talk about getting rich; he demonstrates how to accomplish it. This book helped me change my thinking about money and set attainable goals. The parts on passive income streams and real estate investments were very insightful. If you're ready to take control of your financial destiny, this is the book for you.

David Martinez, a Small Business Owner

"Tim Wealth's book is a must-read for everyone looking to develop wealth. 'What Makes Rich' provides practical guidance based on real-world situations. I really enjoyed the portions on diversifying revenue streams and harnessing technology to maximize rewards. Whether you're just getting started with your finances or want to enhance your investment game, this book has something for everyone."

Emily Chen, Freelancer

"If you're weary of living paycheck to paycheck and want to achieve financial freedom, look no further than Tim Wealth's 'What Makes Rich'. This book taught me the value of investing in myself and my future. Tim's advice on diversifying investing portfolios and reducing risk was invaluable. I've already started adopting his suggestions, and I can clearly see a difference in my financial situation. Get this book now—you won't regret it!"

Michael Thompson, an IT professional

"Tim Wealth's 'What Makes Rich' is a breath of new air among personal finance books. Instead of making sweeping claims of instant achievement, Tim provides actionable advice that anyone can implement. This book covers everything from defining SMART financial objectives to creating an effective budget. I especially loved the chapter on breaking limiting assumptions about money—it was just what I needed to hear. Do yourself a favor and get a copy today!"

Jessica Davis, Educator

"As a new college graduate, I felt intimidated by the prospect of managing my funds and generating wealth. Fortunately, I discovered 'What Makes Rich' by Tim Wealth. This book acted as a crash lesson in personal finance, teaching me everything from budgeting to investing. Tim's writing style was straightforward and succinct, making difficult financial ideas easier to understand. Whether you're just starting off or want to enhance your financial game, I definitely suggest this book!"

Alex Miller, A Recent Graduate.

"I've read a lot of personal finance books, but 'What Makes Rich' by Tim stands out above the rest. His easy writing style and practical recommendations make this book an absolute must-read for anyone trying to improve their financial status. The chapter on creating passive income streams was extremely enlightening and prompted me to look into new ways of generating wealth. Trust me, you will not be sorry to add this book to your library!"

Samantha Lee, Marketing Professional

This book is a goldmine of practical advice for anyone trying to take charge of their financial situation. This book covers it all, from dispelling popular money myths to providing step-by-step guidelines for stock market investing. I really loved Tim's emphasis on the value of financial education and lifelong learning. If you're ready to quit living paycheck to paycheck and start earning real wealth, get yourself a copy of this book!"

Daniel Kim, Software Engineer

"I've always been interested in personal finance, but I struggled to locate tools that spoke to me—until I discovered 'What Makes Rich' by Tim Wealth. This book is game-changing! Tim's straightforward counsel and real-world examples make difficult financial concepts simple to understand. Whether you're a complete beginner or an experienced investor, this book has something for everyone. I have already recommended it to every one of my friends and relatives!"
Rachel Patel, Graphic Designer

"In a world full of get-rich-quick schemes and financial gurus promising instant success, Tim Wealth's 'What Makes Rich' is a breath of fresh air." Tim's straightforward approach to personal finance cuts through the clutter and provides concrete advice that works. I loved the emphasis on long-term wealth creation and the value of establishing a solid financial basis. If you're serious about obtaining financial freedom, do yourself a favor and get this book—you won't be disappointed!"
Kevin Jones, Sales Manager

Acknowledgement

Writing a book on achieving financial freedom is a journey that requires support, inspiration, and guidance from many individuals and resources. I am deeply grateful to all those who have contributed to the creation of this book, "What Makes Rich: Money Mindset on Planning, Budgeting, Saving, and Investing to Gain Financial Freedom".

First and foremost, I want to express my gratitude to my family for their unwavering support and encouragement throughout this endeavor. Your belief in me fueled my determination to complete this project.

I extend my heartfelt thanks to my mentors and advisors, whose wisdom and guidance have been invaluable on my path to financial literacy and independence. Your insights have shaped the content of this book and enriched its message.

To the financial experts, authors, and educators whose work inspired me and informed my understanding of money management and wealth-building principles, I owe a debt of gratitude. Your ideas have served as a guiding light for readers seeking to take control of their financial futures.

I am grateful to the readers and supporters of my podcasts and social media channels, whose engagement and feedback have fueled my passion for spreading financial education and empowerment.

Lastly, I would like to thank my team, whose dedication and expertise have brought this book to life. Your professionalism and commitment to excellence have made the publishing process rewarding.

To everyone who has contributed, whether in a significant or minor way, to the making of this book, I express my deepest appreciation. May the wisdom presented in these pages inspire and empower readers as they begin their path toward achieving financial freedom and fulfillment.

Gratefully yours,

Tim Wealth

Contents

DISCLAIMER	III
ABOUT THE AUTHOR	IV
SEE WHAT PEOPLE ARE SAYING ABOUT THIS BOOK	VI
ACKNOWLEDGEMENT	XI
CONTENTS	XIII
INTRODUCTION	XV
SHAPING YOUR FINANCIAL FUTURE	XV
CHAPTER 1	1
MONEY TALKS: WHAT'S YOUR MONEY SAYING?	1
CHAPTER 2	21
DREAM BIG, PLAN SMART	21
CHAPTER 3	70
BUDGETING: MORE THAN JUST PENNIES AND DIMES	70

CHAPTER 4	111
GROWING YOUR CASH STASH	111
CHAPTER 5	137
FUTURE-PROOFING YOUR WALLET	137
CHAPTER 6	172
WHEN LIFE THROWS YOU A CURVEBALL	172
CHAPTER 7	192
KEEPING YOUR MONEY GAME STRONG	192

Introduction

Shaping Your Financial Future

"If we command our wealth, we shall be rich and free. If our wealth commands us, we are poor indeed." –Edmund Burke

My wife and I recently made a huge financial choice. We were considering making the largest purchase of our lives. It had been on the radar for a while, and the time seemed to have come. We had several chats. We discussed our desires, hopes, and potential outcomes.

As you might guess, I ran the numbers, and we reviewed our financial strategy. We revisited our financial objectives, some of which had shifted, while others had become more pressing. I conducted several scenarios to simulate the consequences of such a purchase. I spoke with others, including financial specialists and trusted loved ones, to ensure that my readings were not unduly emotional.

Together, we questioned how such a purchase would affect our retirement security. What is our current cash flow? Would having to finance the purchase give us unnecessary stress? Could we continue saving for the kids' college? How does this affect our generous intentions? The questions poured down relentlessly.

These are tough questions, but the answers we provide them are critical. We went through the financial planning process again, and not for the first time, but here we were. Again, we must identify our beliefs, evaluate our goals, track our progress, and use those factors to lead our decision-making.

The results, while not perfect, were positive. We could do it. We chatted some more. Numbers aren't life. We understood the role that emotions and desire were playing. Together, we discussed danger, stress, health, children, and the future.

We made an offer, apprehensive but confident after a few months of running predictions. I hit submit; the email went out; the offer was made, and we waited.

I'm sharing this with you since it reminded me how vital financial planning is. It is a dynamic, never-ending process that extends far beyond investments and rewards. Indeed, it could be argued that, without a plan, returns are merely numbers.

Financial planning is life, and it acknowledges that we must make financial decisions throughout our lives. It is about making deliberate choices. It is about being proactive so that we can take advantage of opportunities when they arise. It is being tethered to something rather than being cut adrift in endless oceans beckoning for consumption. This is waiting, which is also the exercise of patience.

The year is still running, making it a great time to examine your financial condition and set goals for the next years. This is especially true for people who have fixed wages and analyze their monthly income and expenses to ensure they are on track with their financial goals for saving and investing.

Typically, financial planning takes place at the beginning of each year. While performing an annual assessment of your money is beneficial, it's important to remember that financial planning is an ongoing activity, not a onetime thing.

Financial planning goes beyond simply tracking income and expenses; it entails taking actions to ensure a solid financial future in the long run.

Whether you are nearing retirement, in the middle of your career, or just starting, it is critical to think about and plan for your future. Psychologists frequently delay retirement planning for a variety of reasons, including extensive training, hefty student loan payments, and the time commitment required to create and run a practice.

What Should I Expect from This Book?

You undoubtedly had a plan in place for the most important moments in your life. Your wedding, for example, had a timeframe, a budget (even if you were overspent with that last-minute table for extended family), and required compromise and conversation. Smart financial planning adheres to the same idea.

This book will help. It will walk you through the steps necessary to establish a personal financial plan and get your money in order. From the groceries you need to the retirement you want and the looming car repair bill, these ideas help you reconcile long-term goals with short-term desires, as well as the unforeseen occurrences that occur along the road.

This book provides a solid foundation upon which you can construct and alter your life. These ideas will assist you in planning your finances for the future.

Your Money Mindset Shapes Your Finances

The principles of personal finance are simple. Spend less than you earn. Invest for the future. Don't buy anything you don't need.

However, as everyone who has ever set a financial goal can attest, putting those guidelines into action is far more difficult. The myths we tell ourselves limit our ability to make financial changes. We worry about things that should not be a concern. And, oh my goodness, we battle to stay within our grocery budget.

Understanding your money mindset and where it came from enables you to change it. Just like you would enter your coordinates into a navigator before embarking on a journey, you should be aware of and comprehend your existing financial beliefs.

As you change your thinking, knowing where you started helps you realize how far you've gone. It's like looking at the navigator and seeing you've already traveled 200 miles. However, the difference with money is that it is a lifelong journey. We never actually arrive at our destination. We just keep increasing. The objective is the trip.

A money mindset is your distinct and specific set of core beliefs about money and how it functions in the world.

It is your attitude towards money. Your money mindset influences what you believe you can and cannot accomplish with money, how much money you believe you are allowed, entitled, and able to make, how much you can and should spend, how you handle debt, how much money you give away, and your capacity to invest confidently and successfully. Your financial perspective shapes your attitude towards individuals, both affluent and poor. Do you believe that poor people are good and virtuous, the salt of the earth, hence it is preferable to be like them?

The way you conduct financial talks reveals another aspect of your money mindset: do you feel vulnerable and afraid, or confident and in control? Are you comfortable asking questions - either yes, since you feel safe asking, or not because you're bashful and embarrassed? Do you have an underlying belief that money is a man's world and women shouldn't be concerned about it?

What's remarkable about our money mindset is that this core set of beliefs is stored in our unconscious mind. And it can remain dormant. However, becoming a close observer of your thoughts, feelings, bodily reactions, and interactions with money allows you to become conscious of your present set point and modify your thinking.

"Positive Thinking" Rather "Money Thinking"

Many people experience worry and anxiety while discussing money. Whether it's struggling to pay bills, dealing with debt, or worrying about financial stability, money-related stress can hurt our mental health and overall well-being.

When attempting to better your financial status, one of the most difficult challenges you will face is not related to money, but rather to your thinking. So, remember that the power of positive thought should not be underestimated.

Stress, particularly financial stress, is frequent; nevertheless, you can reduce the impact by making a conscious decision to focus on the good. This is usually easier said than done, so I'll give you some of the advice in this book to help you keep your mind and money on track:

Set reasonable goals. Take some time to sit down and carefully consider your financial goals. Set yourself up for success by breaking things down into manageable steps. Mastering one tiny step at a time can keep you motivated to achieve your overall financial objective.

Celebrate your achievements. Allow yourself to be proud of your accomplishments, no matter how tiny they may appear. Congratulations on adhering to your monthly budget or even taking the initiative to construct a monthly budget. The satisfaction you derive from these accomplishments will enable you to build on your triumphs.

Accept that you are not flawless. You will experience difficulties that threaten to derail you. These are an unavoidable aspect of life. However, regardless of when or where you become diverted, you do not have to quit and acknowledge failure. It's acceptable to make mistakes. For example, "Today I am thankful for _____." Make a habit of forcing yourself to finish this statement with a different word each day. This allows you to shift your emphasis from what you don't have to what you do have. This is an excellent exercise for when you're feeling overwhelmed or discouraged. It's a simple exercise that will allow you to step back and reevaluate your priorities.

Create an abundance mindset. An abundant mindset is the concept that there is plenty for everyone and that we can bring abundance into our lives by focusing on what we desire rather than what we lack. By adopting an abundance attitude, you begin to see opportunities where you previously saw problems. This can aid in attracting more money and financial success to your life.

Always say positive things. Positive affirmations are phrases that we tell ourselves to assist us change our thinking and beliefs. When it comes to money, positive affirmations can help you conquer your concerns and anxieties while also cultivating a more positive outlook. For example, you might use words like "I am abundant and prosperous" or "Money comes easily and effortlessly to me" to attract more money into your life.

However, having a money attitude and positive thinking alone will not guarantee financial success. It must be accompanied by action and sound financial practices. Positive thinking and understanding a money mindset can help you develop a growth mindset and overcome limiting beliefs, but it is also critical to take actual measures toward financial independence. We all have our financial tales, which are a combination of how we were raised, the successes and failures we've faced, and our future goals. In this book, we'll delve into these stories, questioning the myths and mindsets that keep us stuck. We'll then start from scratch, defining attainable goals, mastering budgeting, and discovering the secrets to building and protecting our wealth.

Money is more than just numbers; it represents freedom, security, and the power to live your greatest life. So, buckle up! You're about to go on a trip that will not only shift your perspective on money but also provide you with the tools you need to attain the financial future you've always desired.

PART 1
Getting Real with Money

Chapter 1

Money Talks: What's Your Money Saying?

"Rule No.1 is never lose money. Rule No.2 is never forget rule number one."– Warren Buffett

Nobody is completely reasonable when it comes to money. We do not construct and stick to a budget or save money every paycheck even though we believe it would be beneficial. We know we need a financial plan, but we put off the necessary work; somehow, it never happens. We spend too much out of carelessness or enthusiasm and too little out of guilt. Our financial decisions frequently cause us to feel ashamed.

It's worth considering money as something you have a complicated relationship with. Your money (and, more broadly, your finances) is not a static item but rather a collection of data points, difficulties, and opportunities that you circle, interact with, and form opinions about. You make financial decisions that affect your financial condition, influencing your sentiments and future behaviors. And it is a bond that develops over a lifetime.

Money may be a difficult topic. Talk to a hundred people, and you'll receive as many diverse viewpoints on everything from savings to investing to tax breaks - many of those perspectives are strongly held.

Like love and religion, money and finance shape many people's daily lives. We all grow up learning various things about money. Experiences of poverty or loss shape some ideas, whereas others are more optimistic and affected by favorable economic conditions and great role models.

Whatever forces shape your "money beliefs," you can be confident that they impact your life and worldview. It is critical to acquire more than just knowledge about money and economics; you must also foster awareness of your thoughts and feelings.

In this chapter, we will look at a few methods you might investigate your personal money beliefs, and as you read, you will discover how these ideas influence how you approach life and your financial goals.

Money Beliefs: How They Shape Us

Martha was raised in a low-income home. Her parents were constantly concerned about money, and she came to believe that money was rare and difficult to obtain. As a result, Martha adopted a scarcity attitude and was constantly cautious about spending money, even when it was essential.

She was overjoyed to finally have a consistent paycheck when she started her first job after college. However, her scarcity mindset made it impossible for her to enjoy her newly acquired financial stability. She continued to live frugally and was hesitant to invest or spend money on things that could improve her standard of living.

Martha didn't realize the value of investing and spending money sensibly until she met a financial expert who helped her change her perspective. With her fresh perspective, she could set financial goals, create a budget, and make sound financial decisions to help her reach her long-term goals.

Martha learned the value of a money-conscious mindset and behavior from this encounter. She realized that by changing her attitudes and practices, she could get control of her financial situation and create a better life for herself.

Money is an essential element of our lives and influences us in various ways, including our views and behaviors. Our money psychology greatly impacts our financial health and can predict whether we will succeed in achieving our financial objectives.

To understand why you feel like you do about money, you must first consider where those feelings originate. Did you grow up in a modest household emphasizing thrift as the only way to reach true security? Were you affected by a culture that encouraged outward displays of wealth?

How and where you grew up, as well as your life events, all impact how you think and feel about money.

According to a study by America First Credit Union, "49% of Millennials turn to their parents for financial advice." Regarding money and finance, parents are one of the most important belief influencers because they are typically in charge of passing down views shaped by their own experiences.

However, parents are not the only influencers. Friends and other social groups can have an impact, and cultural views can influence our financial outlook in various ways. Some communities, for example, oppose openly discussing one's finances, but others are "freer" with such conversations and regard money as a completely natural topic.

It may surprise you to learn that religious beliefs have a significant impact on our money views or "scripts," with one study revealing that "the fear of hell is more potent for economic growth than the prospect of heaven" and that "higher rates of religious beliefs stimulate growth because they help to sustain aspects of individual behavior that enhance productivity."

Knowing how and why you believe certain ideas about money is a critical first step toward understanding your financial behavior.

Healthy vs Unhealthy Money Beliefs

Because our finances significantly impact our quality of life, it's critical to understand whether your money beliefs positively or negatively impact your behavior.

A good money belief reduces tension while motivating and encouraging you to achieve your life goals. A negative belief will produce dread and discomfort, leading you to behave in ways detrimental to your financial health.

Financial psychology is a relatively young research subject, yet it has been discussed for decades. The Financial Psychology Centre defines Financial Psychology as a growing field that connects people's attitudes and feelings about money to how they handle it.

This is an essential field of study, especially given the unforeseen events of 2020. Last year's American Psychological Association's Stress in America poll states that "nearly 2 in 3 adults (64%) say that money is a significant source of stress in their life."

The influence of this stress on financial decisions, such as whether to pursue additional education on topics such as correct tax compliance, retirement planning, and investment strategies, is beginning to be appreciated in a broader framework. Unhealthy money ideas tend to deter people from seeking the necessary information and training, and they can cause individual and society harm in various ways.

For example, a culture that fosters widespread "money anxiety" can quickly become a self-fulfilling prophecy for the national economy and the people living within it. As more people question the legitimacy of their financial intelligence and the integrity of the institutions that handle their money, investment markets become more volatile, and people make fear-based decisions that may harm them (and their country) in the long term.

This is why developing a healthy money mindset is critical for your identity and your role as a citizen in an interconnected economy. Although it may not seem like it most of the time, your financial decisions influence how your entire community looks and approaches money and associated regulations.

Rather than feeling overwhelmed by this burden of duty, Financial Psychologists recommend that you use it to improve your financial health and handle money concerns together, as you are not alone. Seeking good advice and correct information does not have to be an unpleasant personal responsibility, but rather a civic duty and legal right shared equally by everyone in your native nation.

Healthy money values are based on the notion that, while circumstances change regularly, strong financial practices are a dependable approach to weather any obstacles that may arise. They also emphasize money as a component of your life rather than making it a major element of daily living.

For example, money may be an incredible social force. "By spending money wisely, you can help to create better relationships" For example, you could use the money to arrange a family vacation and create wonderful memories that will last a lifetime. Money can be used to produce all kinds of entertaining arrangements that bring you closer to your family and friends. Finally, healthy ideas about money revolve around the idea that it is a tool to pursue a happier, more fulfilling life rather than a weapon or a mysterious force beyond our control.

Money Myths You Should Never Believe

Abundant false information is available, and believing some of it can cost you money. Other people may steer you in the wrong direction, or it might be what you tell yourself. Whatever the origins, believing these beliefs could jeopardize your financial health. We will look at several prevalent money misconceptions that are not just personal but widely believed by most people. These fallacies leave many people financially trapped and unable to achieve their goals.

Myth 1: Debit Is Always Far Better Than Credit

Credit cards are sometimes blamed for encouraging people to accumulate debt, yet they can also provide numerous benefits:

Many credit cards provide rewards such as cashback, petrol discounts, and other perks.

Developing and maintaining a healthy credit history is critical to your financial health. One simple method to accomplish this is to use credit cards, keep your balances low, and pay your bills on time.

Many credit cards provide purchase protection, making them an ideal payment method for large purchases.

Myth 2: Buy A Home at Any Cost

Owning a home provides more independence and flexibility but entails greater responsibility and maintenance expenditures. For many people, particularly those who want to move around frequently, don't want to worry about the cost of house upkeep, or can't afford the higher upfront expenditures of homeownership, renting may be a better option.

Myth 3: Investing Is Just for The Rich

Anyone with a small savings can invest. Whether it's in a short-term certificate account, a long-term IRA, or even the stock market, there's a plan for everyone. A sensible investing strategy can be the most effective method to put your money to work and achieve financial freedom.

Myth 4: My Partner Handles the Finances, So I Don't Need to Know About Money

Regardless of whether their partner is involved, every adult should be in charge of the family's finances. While one couple can actively handle the family's finances, both must be aware of the situation and capable of handling household costs and assets in an emergency.

Myth 5: Credit Cards Can Get You Through Any Financial Crisis

Using credit cards to get through a financial emergency is a wonderful way to end up in deep debt. Depending on your situation, you may not be able to pay your credit cards on time, and with interest and late fees, you could spend far more than you charged in the first place. Credit cards should not be used during a true financial emergency, such as a job loss, divorce, or major sickness. Starting an emergency fund with three to six months' worth of living expenses is important so you're ready for unexpected catastrophes.

Myth 6: I Am Too Young to Think About Retirement

The earlier you begin establishing your retirement fund, the less you'll have to contribute each month, and the more you'll save by the time you retire. Give yourself a comfortable, stress-free retirement by maxing out your 401(k) contributions and taking advantage of company contributions (where available). If your workplace does not provide a retirement plan, you can open an IRA or explore alternative higher-interest accounts.

Myth 7: I Have Enough Money and Don't Need to Budget

Budgeting applies to everyone, not just those who live paycheck to paycheck. Even people with six-figure salaries can easily go into debt if they don't have a realistic budget. A budget will compel you to consider where and how much money you spend in each category (home, car, subscriptions, etc.) and will assist you in making prudent financial decisions.

Myth 8: Scarcity

Scarcity is at the heart of many money misconceptions. It is a damaging worldview that underpins all limiting views about money. Unfortunately, previous generations have passed this thinking down to us, having lived through revolutions, wars, famines, and the Great Depression.

Previously, those limiting beliefs benefited them because there wasn't enough to go around. However, there has been significant improvement over the previous century, and as a community, we have devised smart solutions to shortages.

The truth is that our world is full of riches. Although humans tend to focus on areas of scarcity, such as energy obtained from fossil fuels, energy is abundant in the sun, wind, water, biofuels, and geothermal energy from the earth's core.

Our cognitive-negative bias leads us to focus on shortages. This powerful behavior lets us emphasize bad information and experiences more than favorable ones.

To break the scarcity mindset, you must overcome your negative bias by intentionally focusing on the areas of abundance rather than lack. This can be difficult because we tend to pay greater attention to bad information. The good news is that you can take action to make things easier.

Myth 9: Time Equals Money

If you work and are paid by the hour, you may believe that charging a high hourly rate is the only way to get wealthy. But how feasible is that?

Exchanging your time for money will always be a restricted strategy for wealth growth, regardless of your intelligence or skill. This is because the quantity of money people are willing to pay you is constantly limited and defined by the market. Furthermore, your working hours will be limited because we only have 24 hours every day.

The concept that time is essential for wealth creation excuses us if we are not affluent. We can then use the justification that we've spent our time on more essential things, such as family and friends, creating excellent relationships, and caring for ourselves. We may be confident that we did not give up our family or lifestyle to get wealthy.

However, the creators of Facebook, Groupon, and Pinterest have made large fortunes in relatively short periods. Only individuals who put their time and money to work will see their living standards grow without jeopardizing other important aspects of their lives.

Myth 10: Money Will Not Make You Happy

It's difficult to disagree with the adage, "There's more to life than money." There are certainly numerous experiences with deep value and worth that cannot be had solely through purchasing them. But does this imply that money will not make you happy?

According to research, money can make us happier. Elizabeth Dunn, a Canadian researcher, and her colleagues discovered that spending as little as $5 per day on someone else can greatly improve your happiness. In other words, generosity brings happiness, and having money permits you to be even more generous.

Not having enough money to provide food, shelter, and clothing for yourself and your family can be distressing. Stress and anxiety often do not allow for happiness. Even those who look to be wealthy can experience stress if they have financed their lifestyle with a high degree of debt.

Your motive plays a vital role in determining whether or not money can make you happy. Someone with a nicer home, a more attractive girlfriend, or a larger yacht will always be there. But if you want more options, be more generous and bountiful, be free to pursue your heart's desires, have fantastic experiences, learn, and live life to the fullest, money may help.

Your underlying belief framework is quite essential. It drives your motivation and might be based on scarcity and competition or abundance and generosity.

After you've been completely aware of these myths, consider how you might overcome this negative belief system that has long stood between you and abundance.

Overcoming Limiting Financial Beliefs

If you have subconscious money-related beliefs, they will hold you back. Especially the money misconceptions I just discussed. If you believe that money is evil, difficult to obtain, not destined to be yours, too rare to obtain, or unworthy of it, opportunities to obtain it will not arise for you. The only solution is to confront and conquer your limiting ideas. If you say you want to make money, but your heart does not agree, you will struggle to become wealthy.

Here, I will discuss how you can overcome your limiting views about money and change your perspective on making, saving, spending, and investing money.

Examine Your Childhood Financial Culture

"It's helpful to evaluate your current relationship with money by reflecting, without judgment, on your early financial culture." This enables you to objectively analyze the trends and behaviors that shaped your financial beliefs and perspectives without causing you any difficulties. This self-awareness can assist you in identifying negative money scripts that may hinder you from meeting your financial objectives. Once you've acknowledged your experiences and beliefs, you may go forward with healthy behaviors and perspectives on using money as a wealth-building tool.

Digging deep promotes self-awareness. Every family has its own money culture, encompassing their financial views, spending, saving, and investing, and the language they used to discuss money. Understanding your family's money culture is more than eliminating undesirable behaviors and restricting ideas; it may also help you uncover the positive behaviors and attitudes it instilled in you. Finally, it can help you notice when old thought patterns arise, allowing you to distance yourself from them and replace them with more effective money beliefs. You may rewire your brain to believe that "what you sow is what you will reap", even if your upbringing taught you, for instance, that "money doesn't grow on trees".

Uncouple Your Emotions

Emotions play an important role in financial decision-making; frequently impacting choices more than you realize. Fear, greed, and worry can impair our judgment, leading to rash or foolish financial judgments. Fear of missing out (FOMO) can lead to rash investing decisions without adequate study or due diligence. Similarly, anxiety and stress can cause people to overpay or make unnecessary purchases.

Your past money experiences also influence your feelings towards money. If you were raised in a family that regarded material goods as a status symbol, you are more prone to spend impulsively to keep up with your peers or maintain a specific lifestyle. Remove the ego from possessions, and the superiority complex from financial achievement, and adopt an abundant mindset on giving and receiving. Emotions can be great motivators for making financial decisions but can also obscure your judgment and lead to poor choices.

Remove Monetary Blind Spots

Any financial blind spots that affect the way you view money in your life must be removed. Money blind spots include fear of failure, lack of confidence, and self-doubt. These feelings can lead to self-sabotage and a reduction in earning potential since you avoid taking chances that could result in bigger financial rewards.

Identifying your financial blind spots will help you develop a more optimistic and abundant mindset. Recognizing and confronting negative ideas and beliefs might help you adopt a more optimistic and growth-oriented mindset. Suppose you have a limiting mindset that you are unworthy of producing a lot of money. In that case, you may unknowingly shut yourself off from possibilities that could lead to financial success, and the thought becomes a self-fulfilling prophecy. What are your beliefs about what is possible, and how will they aid you in the future?

Rewrite Your Story

Humans tell themselves stories on repeat without questioning whether they are true. One example is, "I need more money to plan the future I truly desire." You can see how this would prevent someone from gaining money because they don't understand why they desire it. Fueled by restrictive beliefs and harmful stories, a pessimistic mindset tells entrepreneurs they cannot achieve money right now. But they can do it now.

You need to redefine your mindset. Tell yourself a better story. Your fresh narratives may include, "I have enough money to begin planning for my future," as well as, "I have all the ingredients to create huge financial success." Even "If anyone can do it, I can." Be your cheerleader by making up stories and seeing them through to the point where you believe them. This will keep you motivated and focused even in the face of obstacles. It also promotes open-mindedness, curiosity, and creativity, which can lead to new ideas and sources of money. Conversely, you may unwittingly turn down prospects for financial success if you have a negative outlook or a sense of scarcity.

Implement Realistic Solutions

Establish accountability for taking action to achieve your financial goals. Set calendar reminders to monitor bank accounts and spreadsheets, collaborate with a professional, form a money mastermind support group, or tie metrics in your business to specific success milestones to celebrate. Make money your primary priority, knowing that you can and will discover ways to make more. Remind yourself that if others can find a solution, you can too.

Realistic methods to eliminate restrictive financial attitudes require a combination of self-awareness, practical actions, and patience. What you do not do is equally significant to what you do. Don't let your family of origin or emotional triggers keep you bound in a scarcity mindset, preventing you from achieving the degree of riches you desire daily. Do not listen to doubters, bad media, or people who have given up on their financial goals. Hang out with individuals finding ways to go forward, and you will, too.

Overcome your limiting thoughts about money and achieve the income of your dreams while maintaining mental and emotional freedom. Revisit your past to determine the source of your beliefs, then identify triggers, uncouple from unproductive emotions, and eliminate your money blind spots. Next, rewrite your stories and use realistic and practical answers. Begin a journey of consciously changing your mindset about what you can earn, spending, keeping, and investing.

So far, in this chapter, we've covered money beliefs and how they shape our lives. We also discussed common money fallacies and why they should be debunked. I also discussed overcoming these money fallacies that may have instilled negative beliefs in you.

In the following chapter, I'll walk you through the various tactics needed to achieve your financial dreams, including a full guide to defining and attaining goals.

Let us journey together.

Chapter 2

Dream Big, Plan Smart

"If your dreams don't scare you, they aren't big enough." **Lowell Lundstrum**

Most people fail to reach their full potential because they do not dream large enough. They set overly modest expectations and then wonder why they never reach greatness. I always remind myself that "to live an outstanding life, you must first visualize your objectives before acting to realize them."

I wish I had listened to myself earlier and learned to dream big and make things happen sooner.

I understand that dreaming large might be challenging, since we frequently perceive it as an impossible goal reserved for a select few. However, anyone can have huge ambitions and turn them into reality. All you and I need is some hard work and determination.

When it comes to achieving financial objectives, it's wonderful to dream, but it's also necessary to plan precisely and strategically. So, in this chapter, I'll take you through the symbiotic relationship between thinking large and planning smart, revealing the tactics and insights required to navigate the path to financial success.

Set Financial Goals That Motivate You

Setting financial objectives is crucial to obtaining financial success. Whether you're saving for a down payment on a new home or hoping to retire early, having a plan of action will help you achieve your goals most effectively.

Setting financial objectives is a great strategy to increase wealth, provide direction and purpose, and keep you on track to financial success. Setting financial objectives can also encourage and inspire you because they provide concrete measures for success.

You may decide that your financial goal is to save for retirement, pay off debt, invest in assets, or do something else entirely. Setting a financial goal is the first step towards dramatically improving your financial well-being. Every milestone reached and dollar saved will provide additional inspiration and drive, allowing your financial objectives to become a practical reality over time.

Setting short term, mid-term, and long-term financial goals is vital to financial stability. You will spend more than necessary if you aren't working towards a defined goal. You'll then fall short when you need money for unexpected expenses, let alone when you want to retire. You may become trapped in a cycle of credit card debt and believe that you will never have enough money to get fully insured, leaving you more susceptible than necessary to deal with some of life's major hazards.

Even the most prudent individual cannot prepare for every disaster, as the globe discovered during the pandemic and as many families continue to learn each month. Thinking ahead allows you to sort through potential outcomes and do your best to prepare for them. This should be an ongoing process so that you can adapt your life and ambitions to the changes that will inevitably occur.

Anyone with the confidence to set lofty financial objectives and devise a strategy to attain them can realize their financial fantasies. The trick is to begin small and work your way up. Set short-term financial objectives first, then work your way to larger financial goals.

Make careful to track your success regularly so that you may adjust your plans as needed. When you have the confidence to set huge financial goals and work hard, you can achieve them - just take one step at a time.

The Advantages of Financial Goal Setting

One of the major benefits of creating financial goals is that it keeps you focused and motivated. Having an end goal helps you stay on track and avoid distractions. It also increases discipline because you have something tangible to work towards and can use it as motivation when times are tough. Goal setting also provides clarity and direction. You understand exactly what you're working towards and can arrange your efforts accordingly. This enables more efficient expenditure since you can prioritize what needs to be done immediately against what can wait till later. It also helps you keep organized because all your plans are written out before you. Setting financial objectives will help you improve your spending habits. Having a goal in mind makes it easier to find areas where you can save money, whether it's cutting back on takeaway or skipping certain luxury purchases.

You'll become more aware of how and where you spend your money and think twice before purchasing something unneeded or pricey.

Recognize that limitation can be helpful in the long run, leading to increased wealth accumulation. Assume you have set a goal to save for a down payment on a house. You'll understand how to avoid wasting money on unnecessary purchases and instead focus on saving it.

By prioritizing your spending, you may determine what is most important to you financially and make decisions accordingly. You will be able to save for your future goals.

Also, setting financial objectives might assist in lessening stress. Knowing you have a financial plan removes the fear of insufficient money to handle bills or emergencies.

It might also help you feel more secure about your financial status. Having confidence that you are in charge of your finances provides peace of mind and reduces stress.

Without financial goals, it might be difficult to envision what your future should look like. This may cause worry and indecision while deciding how to spend your money.

You can avoid the sensation of panic by setting financial goals. This will offer you a better direction and purpose for your money, decreasing stress. Just remember to set realistic financial objectives that you can achieve. Setting unrealistic goals can only lead to additional stress and unhappiness in the long run. Setting financial objectives might also help you reach financial independence. This entails having enough money to cover your daily costs and accumulate riches for the future.

Financial independence also entails the ability to make decisions without worrying about money. For example, you could take a career hiatus to spend time with your family or work on a passion project.

You will also be less likely to go into debt since you have developed good money management skills by defining and achieving your goals.

Setting these goals will assist you in making the most of your income while avoiding unforeseen surprises. All of this can lead to more financial independence in the long term. Finally, creating goals increases your chances of success by forcing you to plan and foresee probable issues.

The importance of creating financial objectives cannot be emphasized. As previously said, the benefits demonstrate the clear effect that goal setting may have on your financial growth.

Creating these goals gives you a feeling of direction and purpose, laying the groundwork for enhanced motivation, effective decision-making, and better money management.

Setting and attaining financial goals can inculcate essential skills and habits that go beyond money and positively impact other aspects of life.

Finally, embracing financial goal setting is an investment in yourself and your future, allowing you to take charge of your financial situation and work towards a more secure, affluent, and satisfying life.

3 Rules for Setting Financial Goals

When embarking on this path, it is critical to establish goals. When learning to develop financial objectives, three important factors must be considered. Your financial objectives should be:

1. Measurable

How will you know your development if you can't quantify it? You must clearly describe what you intend to do, by when, and what you must do each week or month to achieve your ultimate goal.

2. Realistic

Avoid setting impossible goals for yourself. Yes, your goals should be difficult and outside of your comfort zone, but they should not be foolish or impossible. If saving $5,000 a year is simple for you, why not set a goal of $10,000?

However, setting a goal of $1,000,000 when saving $10,000 is already challenging. Well, you get my point!

3. Written down

The most critical step in financial goal setting is to write your goals down! Putting pen to paper and writing down your goals has a certain charm. Writing down your goals gives them life; seeing them on paper will make them seem even more significant.

Plan Your Financial Goals

Once you've established your goals, it's time to break them down. Imagine you want to save an additional $15,000 over the next 12 months. It might be used to make a down payment on a home, purchase a car, or establish a business.

Whatever you're planning, you'll need to save around $1,250 per month. You already know that money isn't going to just fall into your lap. To achieve this goal, you must fit it into your budget, identify areas where you may cut back, consider ways to potentially improve your income, and make consistent payments to maximize your outcomes.

These actions can significantly help you achieve your $15,000 savings target. But, knowing all this, how do you do it?

Choose one thing or action you will perform at the start of each day to move you closer to your goal. Examples of this one thing could include:

- Making a savings deposit.
- Setting up automated transfers.

- Reading a financial book.
- Checking in with an accountability partner.
- Having a no-spend day.

Even if you fail, doing this one item daily will bring you to your goals over time.

How To Set Financial Objectives That Are Easily Attainable

Unfortunately, many people abandon their goals before they have a chance to make progress. Achieving your objectives is frequently easier stated than done.

However, there is no reason why it cannot be easy. You simply need to understand how to work towards your goals. If you want to be successful in accomplishing your financial goals, you must do the following:

Focus On Your Action Plan, Not The Goal Deadline

Focusing on a deadline can make it appear that what you want to accomplish is so far away that you have plenty of time to complete it "later." However, suddenly, it's too late to do anything.

When you focus on your action plan for the large goals (which you've broken down into chunks and tracked daily, weekly, monthly, or quarterly), you're more likely to do what's necessary to achieve them due to your consistent activities. This will take me to the next point.

Focus On the Deeds Rather Than the Performance

The activities you do are more important than the actual performance. Why? Well, your performance may not always be ideal. Still, the regular activities (such as budgeting, saving money on a schedule, making consistent payments on your credit card or student loans, etc.) can help you improve each time and overall performance.

And that's it. These two factors can make a huge difference in making it easy to achieve your goals.

How to stay motivated when pursuing your financial objectives

So, now that you're ready to set financial objectives, you need to know how to stay motivated to achieve them! It is simple to make or think about a goal, but we all lose the motivation to finish and execute these goals over time. And the truth is that motivation is critical to your success!

Although you will experience setbacks and failures in achieving your financial goals, you must remain focused. Here, I'll give some strategies to help you stay on track and focused on your path to financial success, no matter your obstacles.

1. Establish a reward system

Once you've established your financial goals, you may fall into the trap of working too hard to reach them. You may lose sleep and avoid other activities. Once you've chosen your objective, you might quit spending money on shopping, entertainment, or eating.

Even if you manage to do this for a while, you may find yourself burnt out and ready to overindulge before you realize it. Instead of completely redesigning your life, aim for gradual change that includes benefits. Reward yourself for tiny victories when you achieve them.

Instead of preceding all of your favorite things, set aside a piece of your money for occasional minor splurges. You can reward yourself if you stick to your financial goals at the end of the month or week.

This incentive system will assist you to avoid splurging if you're frustrated during a difficult journey. It will also make saving more enjoyable, rather than a kind of self-punishment for earlier financial mistakes you believe you made.

2. Surround yourself with like-minded individuals

If you want to save a certain amount of money or pay off a certain amount of debt, you need to surround yourself with people who are just as determined. This is one of the most effective strategies to stay motivated. These folks can hold you accountable for your financial goals.

3. Seek personal finance information

Reading personal finance books is an alternative to trial and error for learning about finance. Learning from others' mistakes is far more valuable than learning the hard way. That is why the books are available.

Another approach to learning is to attend personal finance events. You will be more engaged at these events and meet others who share your financial goals and mindset.

These personal finance professionals will be the first to encourage you to prioritize your "why." If you focus on the "why" of your goal and how it will benefit your life and well-being, you will be far more likely to stick to your financial objectives.

Try to shift your focus away from money or earning more money. Instead, let any extra money you earn be a byproduct of your aim. The simplest way to burn out is to focus solely on how much money you want to make rather than on living a better life.

4. Start small

We've all heard about the snowball effect! For example, while it may be logical to tackle your largest debts first, doing so in reverse is better for your mental health because you'll be able to celebrate tiny victories much faster than if you started with your highest sums. This will keep you motivated and thrilled to pursue your long-term financial goals. As you begin to think about your goals, consider how you may structure them such that you can reap the motivational benefits of completing minor victories. Living thrifty (being more conscious of how you spend money) for a while will help you build up those modest victories!

On Your Road To Success

Setting and pursuing financial objectives properly allows you to realize your wildest aspirations, exceed your expectations, and make genuine progress toward financial success.

Vision Board Magic: Seeing Is Achieving

Everyone wants to bring something to life. But what if you can't see it?

It is difficult to gain traction if you lack a vision and cannot define what you want or where to go.

Without a clear vision, guiding your activities in ways that benefit your goals is difficult. It's also difficult to get the help and resources you need.

This is where a vision board comes in.

You may have heard people talk about manifestation, which is the belief that by thinking about your ideal vision, you may bring it into reality. In reality, our dreams do not manifest themselves. It takes work to achieve your goals and reach your full potential.

At the same time, having a specific vision and confidence in your ability to put that vision into reality is beneficial. And from action to reality.

Vision boards are excellent for developing a clear vision and initiating the actual manifestation process.

What exactly are vision boards, and do they work? Vision boards are all about intentions and are an excellent tool to remind yourself of them.

Let's talk about how to develop a vision board for yourself and how to use it once you've made it a reality.

A Vision Board: What Is It?

A vision board is an assembly of pictures or items arranged to assist you in realizing your objectives. This board could be digital or tangible.

Vision boards are very adaptable. They can be used to make a visual depiction of your personal vision statement or to help you achieve your own goals. They are ideal for assisting you in visualizing your ideal existence. However, you can also create a vision board to list your career objectives.

A vision board can be used to outline long-term objectives, such as finishing a five-year plan. Alternatively, you may make a vision board every year.

People typically hang them wherever they can view them frequently when using vision boards. A vision board, for example, could be hung above the mirror you use to get ready in the morning. It will be more appealing to others to display on a wall in a frequently used room.

What Ought to Be Included On A Vision Board?

The possibilities for what can be on a vision board are endless. Add pictures that inspire you or evoke a certain emotion first. When was the last time you viewed a picture or photo that evoked strong emotions in you? What emotions did you experience? Does this sensation fit in with your principles? When considering what to put on your board, you should aim for that.

Quotations that support your vision are also included on vision boards. They can be written by hand, printed and affixed to the board, drawn in calligraphy, or cut into unique shapes using materials like worn-out shirts.

Additionally, sentimental artifacts might be added to a vision board. You can affix these objects to sentimental moments that remind you of your objectives.

There are no restrictions when it comes to creating a vision board. You can try adding it to a board if that's possible. Whether or not it will assist you in realizing your vision is what matters most.

How Do Vision Boards Operate?

You know that thinking about your goals, repeating them, or writing them down on X scraps of paper won't get you there.

What, then, is the purpose of a vision board?

You assemble a board using craft supplies, magazine clippings, and other random objects. How can something so basic assist you in defining and completing your goals? There are some moments when it looks like magic.

It's not quite magic, though.

- Because they serve as a visual reminder of your goals, vision boards are useful tools. This prompt might assist you in maintaining your concentration on your objectives even in the face of difficulties. You may bolster your resolve and boost your drive to act by regularly revisiting and updating your vision board and repeating your goals.
- Vision boards aid in goal clarification. They can then clearly point you toward your goals in several aspects of your life. Thinking about your goals and dreams is necessary while making a vision board. You can better grasp what you want to accomplish by putting your goals into visual form. With this clarity, you may make meaningful goals that align with your vision.
- Vision boards serve as a continual reminder of your top goals. By defining your goals, you might have a deeper understanding of who you are. You can "manifest the things you want" by taking action to obtain them with this visual reminder. Your dream board serves as a helpful reminder of

your values whenever you need to decide life. Consider it a little prod in the correct direction.

- In this sense, vision boards are comparable to journaling. Writing things down helps people make their goals and desires simpler. However, vision boards are ideal for those who would rather see a picture of that goal. They allow you to see your success. By often looking at your vision board, you can immerse yourself in a visual picture of what you want or expect to achieve.

- A vision board contains phrases, images, and symbols that inspire and drive you. This helps form a positive and powerful image in your mind, making it easier to believe in your capacity to achieve your goals. Your board should make you feel happy, excited, and enthusiastic when you look at it. These feelings will help you stay motivated and determined. It reminds you of the possibilities ahead and acts as a visual depiction of your dreams.

- Seeing your aspirations and objectives on your vision board can boost your self-assurance and self-belief. It acts as a continual reminder that you can achieve your objectives. Your self-belief grows when you picture yourself in your ideal situation, which can positively affect your choices and actions.

- It's simple to become sidetracked and lose sight of our objectives in our hectic life. But looking at your vision board daily helps you remember your objectives. It serves as a visual anchor, guiding and reminding you of what's important. It assists you in setting priorities for the activities that align with your vision for your time, effort, and resources.
- Gratitude and optimism are other themes that might be included in a vision board. It is possible to develop an attitude of abundance and appreciation by using sayings, affirmations, or pictures that express thankfulness and an optimistic outlook. Adopting this mindset has the potential to enhance your general state of well-being and draw in further favorable events.

Though a vision board is useful, don't forget that you still need to take inspired action to achieve your objectives. Your actions ultimately make your ideas come true, even though the board serves as a guide and a source of inspiration. By combining the power of visualization with persistent work, tenacity, and grit, you can raise your chances of reaching your financial objectives.

How To Create a Manifesting Vision Board

Making a vision board is simple and enjoyable. Play and be creative with yourself. It's not necessary to overthink the procedure. There is no one you need to impress with your vision board; it is just for you.

By taking the following actions, you may make a tangible vision board that you can display at any place in your house or place of business:

1. Give your vision some clarity.
2. Compile your supplies.
3. Look for pictures and items that symbolize your vision.
4. Set up your supplies.
5. Hang your vision board in a visible location.

Let's dissect each of these actions.

1. Give Your Vision Some Clarity

Thinking about your goals and dreams is necessary while making a vision board. Spend some time crystallizing your vision before you begin crafting. With your board, what do you wish to manifest?

Make your vision as clear as you can. Spend time on this step. It serves as the cornerstone of your whole board. You'll acquire even more detail and clarity as you work on the board.

During this step, avoid using other forms of entertainment to divert your attention, such as talking to family members or watching TV in the background while considering your vision. It's critical to maintain self-awareness while you work to define your goal.

If you find that writing things down helps, you can keep a journal.

2. Compile Your Supplies

Many supplies are needed to create a vision board. You can get by with what you have on hand in certain situations. However, certain components are more crucial than others.

As an example, you will require a board for the base. You can utilize a variety of boards, such as wire boards, whiteboards, and magnetic boards for refrigerators.

Utilizing one of these bases is not required if you don't want to shell out a lot of money for fresh supplies to create your vision board. Alternatively, you could cut a huge piece of cardboard out of a box you already own. Alternatively, buy a sizable poster board at the nearest dollar store.

To add images or other items to the board, you'll also need them. These pictures may be from old postcards, old photos, printed copies of internet images, vintage periodicals and catalogs, and more.

You'll then need something to fasten your belongings to your base. You are free to buy what you would like to utilize or use what you already have. Clips and pins function well. Tape or glue sticks are other options. If you're creating a magnetic board, you can use tiny magnets to hold your pictures in place. You'll also need scissors to help you cut out your photos.

Lastly, a range of craft supplies is required, such as paint, stickers, markers, pens, and other items you wish to utilize to decorate your board. You are free to use these assets in any quantity you choose.

3. Look For Pictures and Items That Symbolize Your Vision

Your supplies have already been assembled. It's time to get them ready to go up on your board. In addition to photos, you can also include quotes on your board. These can be written by hand with a quality pen or marker or printed out.

Are there any objects that bring back memories from your past that evoke the emotion you're imagining? If so, you might want to add it to your board.

You can even include craft supplies like leftover cloth. Alternatively, if it aligns with your objectives, you might incorporate natural elements like tree branches. For example, adding pine needles or leaves can remind you to spend more time outdoors.

4. Set Up Your Materials.

It's time to set up your board using everything you've prepared.

Play around with this step a little. Your layout should inspire you. It doesn't need to be rushed.

Try experimenting with different layout options until you find the best one. This procedure is a component of creating a future vision that is more precise and comprehensive.

By the time you reach this stage, you might find that something is missing. Please feel free to return and add anything more.

Once you're done, use your preferred binding material to secure everything firmly. Take your time securing your belongings. Verify that you're satisfied with it. Changing items around is simple when pins or clips are used. However, altering your mind later will be far more difficult if you're taping or gluing your items.

5. Organize Your Vision Board Such That You Can See It Frequently.

Now is the ideal moment to hang your vision board. Pick a location that makes sense to you. It needs to be daily and freely available.

You could attempt:

- Your refrigerator
- A vacant wall in your cooking area

- An altar
- A reflective surface
- The nightstand you use
- If you work from home, inside your home office

Don't put your vision board in its new location by screwing it too firmly. If you decide to change your mind about the positioning, here it is.

How To Make an Online Vision Board

Anywhere you have an internet-connected device, you can view online vision boards. Additionally, printing or purchasing pricey materials is not necessary.

Here's how to digitally bring your first vision board to life.

1. Select Your Instrument

To make a free vision board, you have a few possibilities. Some people enjoy using it because Pinterest makes it so simple to compile links and images. But Pinterest isn't set up like a conventional goal board. A layout cannot be made the same way as a real board.

Canva is one application that makes creating a digital vision board simple for non-designers. Even if you are not skilled in design, you can still construct a more traditional board with Canvas user-friendly design tools.

2. Where To Find Your Photos

The beauty of using digital tools to create a vision board is that you can use almost any image you choose.

There are tonnes of excellent photos available that are also royalty-free. Searching for precisely what you're searching for on websites like Unsplash or Pixabay is simple.

Images from beloved social media profiles can likewise be used as a source. You can use other people's photographs if you keep your vision board private. Remember that these photographs do not belong to you in terms of copyright. If you want to share your vision board with the public, you must obtain permission.

To further inspire you, try searching for vision board ideas online.

3. Start From Scratch or Utilize a Template.

Online, you may get both premium and free Canva templates. With these templates, creating a visually stunning vision board is much simpler. To complete the process, simply input your photographs and arrange them as desired.

Another option is to begin from scratch. You'll have to decide on your board size if you do. The area where you want to utilize the board the most should determine the size you select. For instance, if you want to primarily view your board as a background or lock screen on your smartphone, you should make it vertical.

4. To Your Digital Vision Board, Add Your Pictures and Sayings

When you're all set, it's time to add your vision board's digital images and quotes.

Pin what you see on the appropriate board when using Pinterest. But you'll need to consider where to put your images, whether you're using Canva or another design program.

Take your time with this phase as you would with a physical vision board. Digital boards have the amazing feature of allowing you to undo any work you are unhappy with. Additionally, you may adjust your phrases and images to ensure that everything fits precisely how you had in mind.

5. Save The Picture

It's time to save and export your file if you are satisfied with how your board looks. It should be noted that this only works with apps such as Canva, as you cannot export a Pinterest board.

You may quickly and easily save and export your image for free inside Canva. You can export a wider variety of file types with a premium account.

What, then, is your file's exportable use? Set it as the backdrop on your computer or as the lock screen for your phone. Alternatively, you may print the board and hang it in your house.

Make sure the size of your board is sufficient for the final printing size if you plan to print it. If a board is too small, printing it at a large scale will make it appear pixelated and fuzzy.

Ideas For Manifestation for Your Vision Board

You now understand how to make a vision board from the ground up. But when you have so much you want to get done, it can be hard to know where to begin.

Let's discuss some manifestation concepts to help you decide what to put on your board.

- **Symbols from trade periodicals**, tools of the trade, and symbols of financial prosperity that indicate career goals
- **Self-care:** Motivational sayings, recollections, calming visuals that promote well-being, and ideas for exercise

- **Love and Relationships:** Sayings that express your beliefs about them, pictures of happy partnerships
- **Optimism:** Visuals that bring you delight, sayings that uplift you, and mental health
- **Travel:** Postcards, pictures of your ideal locations, pictures of trains or airplanes, and pictures of you traveling

Make Use of a Manifest Money Vision Board to Draw Wealth

We all aspire to be financially independent, and creating a vision board can help achieve those aspirations. You can direct your intention and energy towards achieving your financial goals and dreams by putting them into a visual depiction.

I know you know exactly what a vision board is and how to use it to help you reach your objectives. In this section, I'll demonstrate how to use a vision board to attract wealth and achieve financial success.

A Manifest Money Vision Board: What Is It?

A vision board for manifest money is an effective tool for realizing your financial goals. It's a graphic representation that assists you in directing your intention and energy toward realizing your financial aspirations. You can synchronize your subconscious mind with your conscious objectives by making a physical board with words, symbols, and images associated with prosperity and achievement.

A manifest money vision board is predicated on the Law of Attraction, which holds that things attract similar things. You start drawing money and financial success into your life when you surround yourself with positive images and affirmations.

Making a vision board for manifesting money is easy. Here's how to accomplish it:

1. **Establish Your Intentions:** First, clear your financial objectives and preferences. Give precise instructions on how and how much money you wish to create in your life.
2. **Assemble Visual Materials:** Compile images, sayings, and symbols for prosperity, abundance, and financial achievement. You can make your own, print them online, or cut them out of magazines.
3. **Select a Board:** Look for a canvas or board that will serve as the foundation for your vision board. Depending on your preference, you can use a digital platform, a corkboard, or a poster board.

4. **Organize and Adhere:** Position the visual aids on the board in a way that resonates with you. To keep them in place, use tape or glue.
5. **Display And Review:** After creating your manifest money vision board, put it somewhere you'll see it frequently. Spend a few minutes daily visualizing yourself living a wealthy and fulfilling life.

Remember that creating a manifest money vision board won't make you rich overnight. It's a technique that helps you change your perspective and concentrate on abundance. It can assist you with attracting chances, making wiser financial decisions, and taking motivated action toward your objectives when applied consistently and with belief. Hence, make your vision board, have faith in the process, and observe the miracle that is your financial life.

The Manifestation Power of Visualization

I've always thought that visualization had great power. It's amazing how our imaginations can conjure up and materialize the image of what we want. Visualization is a key component in manifesting money, helping us to fulfill our financial goals.

You see, our thoughts and beliefs greatly influence our behaviors and results. We are communicating to the universe that we are prepared to receive financial prosperity when we picture ourselves as prosperous and affluent.

However, why does visualization function? The problem is that our subconscious mind cannot distinguish between reality and imagination. By repeatedly visualizing it, we can educate our subconscious mind to believe that we already possess the wealth we desire. And we act instinctively to bring about the things we genuinely believe in.

In addition, visualization fosters focus and clarity. It is simpler to spot possibilities and take the required actions to accomplish our goals when we clearly understand the financial picture in our heads. It resembles a road map that points us in the direction of achievement.

Here are some strategies for using visualization to attract financial abundance:

- **Make a Vision Board:** A manifest money vision board can visually represent your financial objectives and aspirations. Gather things, sayings, and pictures that symbolize success and plenty, then place them on a board or canvas. Put your vision board somewhere you'll see it every day, and allow it to serve as a source of inspiration and drive for achieving your financial objectives.

- **Engage In Daily Visualization Exercises:** Allocate a short period of time every day to envision yourself as prosperous and accomplished. Shut your eyes and picture what having the money you want would be like. Imagine enjoying financial freedom, owning your ideal house and vehicle, and living in your ideal home. This visualization becomes more realistic as you spend more time in it.
- **Make Use of Affirmations:** Affirmations are effective strategies for reprogramming your subconscious. To reinforce good attitudes about money, create positive affirmations related to abundance, such as "I am attracting wealth into my life" or "Money flows to me easily and effortlessly." Repeat these affirmations every day, especially during your visualization exercise.

How to Make a Vision Board for Manifest Money

Establishing a vision board for manifest money is an effective means of achieving financial prosperity. It is beneficial to visualize our financial aspirations, goals, and desires. Here's how to start drawing wealth into your life by making your manifest money vision board:

1. **Assemble Supplies:** Assemble supplies like magazines, scissors, glue, markers, poster board or corkboard, and any additional decorative objects you wish to utilize.
2. **Define Your Goal:** Before beginning, clearly define your goals for your materialized money vision board. Envision yourself accomplishing your financial objectives and experience the feelings of obtaining the money you want.
3. **Select Words and Images:** Look through periodicals, browse photos on the internet, or print out images that speak to your goals regarding money. Select pictures of opulent objects, idealized travel locales, prosperous businesspeople, or any other symbols of richness and wealth. Choose terms or expressions that speak to your financial objectives and make you feel good.
4. **Put Your Board Together:** Start by positioning and adhering your selected pictures and text to your corkboard or poster board. Consider how each component fits into your goal of manifesting wealth.
5. **Add Personal Touches:** By including your images, sayings, or affirmations, you can personalize and make your manifest money vision board stand out. This can help you feel more

connected to your financial objectives and align the board with your preferences.

6. **Keep it Visible:** Hang your manifest money vision board in your office or bedroom or somewhere else you'll see it often. Your financial objectives will remain top of mind due to this continuous visual reminder, which will also support your manifestation efforts.

7. **Review and Update Frequently:** Allocate a specific period each day to glance at your manifest money vision board for a few minutes. Permit yourself to lose yourself in the feelings and the conviction that your financial goals are already being realized. You can add new photos to your board or change your vision as you approach your objectives.

You are actively utilizing the power of visualization and communicating to the universe that you are prepared to receive financial abundance by making a manifest money vision board. Focus on the big picture while taking motivated steps to reach your financial objectives.

Selecting the Appropriate Words and Pictures for Your Vision Board

Selecting the appropriate pictures and phrases to add to your manifest money vision board is one of the most important parts of the process. This is because the images and phrases we select can arouse powerful feelings and convey precise messages to our subconscious minds.

Here's a step-by-step guide on selecting the ideal pictures and phrases for your vision board:

1. **Be Clear About Your Financial Objectives:** Spend some time outlining your goals before choosing phrases and visuals. Consider what you want in terms of abundance and money. Be precise and put your objectives in writing. You may use this clarity to help you choose the appropriate images and text for your vision board.

2. **Access Your Emotions:** Select words and images that make you feel very favorable feelings. Your desires can be powerfully manifested through the relationship between emotions and visualization. If your ideal home is an opulent beach mansion, look for pictures that bring you happiness, excitement, and contentment as you picture yourself in that lovely setting.

3. **Align With Your Principles:** Using language and imagery that reflect your financial ideals and beliefs is critical. If you think having a positive impact and giving back is important, include pictures of yourself using your riches to make a

difference or reflecting generosity. You can make a vision board that speaks to your actual desires with the support of this alignment.

4. **Think About the Various Facets of Prosperity:** Money is only one of the many facets of abundance. While choosing pictures and phrases, consider additional factors like relationships, health, and personal development. Recall that living an abundant life as a whole results in a more balanced and fulfilling life.

5. **Don't Forget to Personalize Your Vision Board:** Don't forget to include personal touches. These might be sentimental quotations that speak to you, pictures of your loved ones, or handwritten affirmations. Your vision board will have greater meaning and impact when you include these intimate components.

Recall that your vision board is an artistic depiction of your financial objectives and preferences. You can successfully use visualization to materialize money by selecting words and images that create powerful feelings and align with your goals. To stay focused on your money goals, keep your vision board in a conspicuous place and review and update it frequently.

Tracking Progress and Staying Motivated

Tracking your progress and remaining inspired are critical components of using a manifest money vision board successfully. It is critical to have a clear knowledge of how you are progressing towards your financial goals and to remain motivated to continue manifesting wealth. Here are some ways that I find useful for tracking progress and remaining motivated:

1. **Set Specific Goals:** When constructing your manifest money vision board, be clear about your financial objectives. Instead of simply visualizing "more money," define precise goals such as saving a certain amount, earning a certain income, or paying off debts. Setting explicit goals provides something tangible to track and measure your progress against.

2. **Break It Down:** To make your goals more manageable, divide them into tiny, attainable steps. For example, if you aim to save a specific amount, divide it into monthly or weekly savings targets. This makes tracking your progress easier and provides you with a sense of success as you reach each milestone.

3. **Use Visual Clues:** Include visual clues on your manifest money vision board to help you measure your progress

visually. For example, you can illustrate your savings goal with a thermometer-style image and color it in as you approach it. Visualizing your progress can help you stay motivated and focused on your financial goals.

4. **Examine and Reflection:** Take regular breaks to examine and reflect on your manifest money vision board. It is critical to return to your board regularly to remind yourself of your objectives, visualize your success, and renew your faith in your manifestation. Make use of these opportunities to reflect on your progress and, if necessary, reconsider your approach.

5. **Celebrate Milestones:** Recognize your progress and accomplishments along the road. Recognize and appreciate the progress you have achieved. Celebrating your accomplishments not only motivates you but also reinforces the wonderful energy surrounding your manifest money vision board.

Remember that tracking your progress and remaining inspired with your manifest money vision board is a continuous activity. Consistency and intention are essential for attracting money and possibilities into your life. By applying these tactics, I am convinced you will remain motivated and see tangible results in your financial path.

Success Stories of People Who Used Manifest Money Vision Boards

Over the years, I've heard countless success stories of people who employed manifest money vision boards and achieved incredible outcomes. These remarkable stories demonstrate the power of visualization and purpose in creating financial riches. Here are some noteworthy examples:

1. **Susan's Debt-Free Journey:** She was overwhelmed by debt and felt hopeless about her financial situation. Determined to turn things around, she made a manifest money vision board, filling it with images of financial freedom, plenty, and stability. Every day, she visualized herself as debt-free and actively working towards her goals. Susan was amazed by the significant changes in her financial situation after paying off all of her bills within a year.
2. **John's Career Breakthrough:** He had always wanted to start his firm but lacked confidence and resources. He decided to try to materialize money vision boards and started visualizing himself running a prosperous and profitable business. He also added photographs of his ideal clientele, work atmosphere,

and financial goals. John was able to acquire unexpected opportunities, secure money, and effectively launch his business because of persistent visualization and action.

3. **Sarah's Dream Home:** Despite wanting to buy her dream home, she failed to save enough money for a down payment. She made a manifest money vision board, which included images of her perfect home, lavish décor, and a sold sign. Sarah spent time each day visualizing herself in her ideal home and taking action towards her objective. After a few months, she received a substantial raise at work, giving her the financial resources to buy her ideal home.

These success stories indicate that manifest money vision boards are effective when used consistently and with intention. By visualizing their desired outcomes, making clear goals, and taking inspired action, these people were able to actualize their financial wishes and make great changes in their lives.

As you can see, materialized money vision boards may be extremely effective instruments for attracting financial prosperity and success. By using visualization techniques and setting specific objectives, you may harness the power of manifestation and take control of your financial future. So, I encourage you to harness the power of visualization by including a manifest money vision board in your everyday practice. This will bring you the financial success and riches that you deserve. Take charge of your financial future today and begin creating the life you desire.

Break The Goals Down

Do you want to gain control of your finances, reach your goals, and ultimately conquer your budget? It's all about tearing things down! There's no better time than now to start working towards your financial goals. However, setting goals intelligently is essential for preventing overwhelm. Many people wait for specific dates, such as the beginning of the month, the start of a new year, a birthday, or other significant occasions, before taking action. But your money does not wait. For your finances, any date is arbitrary.

While others set many goals, hoping to "eat the elephant" in one fell swoop—a surefire formula for failure and financial overwhelm—we adopt a different approach. If you're ready, I'll lead you through some stages to help you break down and create your targets, allowing you to quickly begin accomplishing those important financial goals.

Discover Your True Self

To attain your financial goals, you must consider the challenges you've faced in the past. Take time to consider why your aspirations have not materialized. This may mean confronting some painful realities, but it is a necessary step towards advancement.

When I first began to review and organize my finances, I identified successful tactics and areas for development. Previously, I set several goals but lacked concentration, making them impossible to achieve. I accept full responsibility and admit that this was entirely my fault. It can be difficult to admit this, but it is an important step.

I used to think, "I'll set ALL of my financial goals RIGHT NOW," which, in my small-mindedness, I thought was perfectly feasible. But, hey, don't quit.

I had shiny object syndrome and couldn't seem to stay in one lane for too long. In a sense, it was a case of decision paralysis. I became overwhelmed by the sheer number of decisions in front of me and simply ignored them. I wasn't breaking down my financial goals; I was attempting to accomplish everything at once.

Embrace Your Failures

When reminiscing on those years of financial hardship, I used to look back at the end of the year and ask, "What did we accomplish this year?" It made me feel as if I was wasting time, wasn't accomplishing my financial goals, and needed to prioritize what was truly important.

So, I needed to take a moment to be completely honest with myself. I have to admit that sometimes the prospect of actually reaching our goals terrified me. What would happen next, right? It dawned on me that I was hiding behind all of these financial ambitions to avoid facing them. And the result was failure in every single one of them.

I let not just myself down, but also my colleagues and those closest to me, by failing to remain focused.

I don't know about you, but I dislike failing at anything—it drives me crazy! And, just so you know, I don't think anyone relishes failing at anything, but there have been a few occasions when playing it safe seemed more comfortable. Believe me; I speak from experience.

Embracing what did not work in the past has helped me break down and reframe my ambitions. It's helped me figure out how to attain my financial goals in the future.

Crush Your Financial Goals

Because I felt deep down that I needed to make a change to reach my financial goals, I embarked on a mission to find a clear way. And, guess what? I finally figured out the solution: narrowing my focus. It's the key to making those goals not only attainable but completely doable!

I resolved not to overburden myself with 'all the goals' and instead concentrate on what I call the "Big 3" goals. When it comes to creating financial objectives, don't be concerned with the time of year. Financial "New Year's resolutions" and similar goals frequently result in disappointment.

Quarterly Financial Goals

Every quarter, I like to track and complete the "Big 3". Once you've accomplished one objective, establish another. There's no need to wait for the new year or month. Just keep the momentum going! The crucial thing is to start with just the Big Three.

I hear you wondering, "Wait, only three goals?! I need significant cash gains (or victories) today! "Three goals seem too few." Let me tell you, I too learned a lot from this experience. It was difficult for me to shift my thinking. How can we set only three goals and fail to attain them?!

Honestly, it felt stupid, and it made me feel like a sell-out because it was so simple. I kept thinking the entire time, "Seriously if I only aim for three, how can I not meet my targets!?" The whole point was to achieve my goals! And, guess what? I could accomplish it with only three aims!

Don't Fall for
The Temptation

Doesn't this sound surprising? You can reach your financial objectives by setting only three! Why bother taking on so many extras? Then came the self-talk: "Well, if I can handle three goals, why not try five?" And with that, I was off to the races again.

I won't bore (or scare) you with the intricacies of my internal thought process because, well, it was just a never-ending loop that I had to figure out in my head.

So, once again, I decided to stay with the Big Three if I wanted to be successful. Trying to accomplish more would be too much, and I needed to keep focused on those three objectives.

The Stretch Goal Challenge can help you reach your financial goals.

So, what happens once you've achieved the Big Three? Do you take a couple of months off? Do you unwind and relax? No way! Once you've had the satisfaction of achieving your financial goals, it's time to take on a new challenge. Go for a stretch goal!

Stretch goals are our most challenging, frightening, and extremely ambitious aspirations. To be honest, we rarely hit them. However, by defining goals, we ensure that we will continue to strive for them in the future. They act as a daily reminder, right in front of us.

In case you're wondering how many Stretch Goals to set, I'll let you guess. Yep! You should limit them to three as well. Focusing on three goals again allows you to divide them down into smaller, more manageable chunks. Suddenly, that big hairy goal doesn't appear as frightening!

Timeframe
Mastery

By breaking down each of our financial targets (the Big 3 and the accompanying Stretch targets) quarterly, monthly, and weekly. This method makes managing our financial objectives much easier.

Using this breakdown approach will reveal what's working, what's not, and what you need to change to get back on track to meet your financial objectives. Remember, it's much easier to change your goals after a difficult week or even a month. If you wait a quarter or a year, you will be left wondering what went wrong (and why you did not meet your goals).

Instead, let us break it down into little, doable chunks. What can you do this week to move closer to your financial objectives? So what about next week? What needs to happen by the end of the month to ensure success?

I realized that if I didn't break down my ambitions into smaller steps, I'd always end up in the same place—failing. So, I decided that failing is not an option this time.

Avoid Financial Derailment

I must say that I am not a fan of failing or making mistakes. This fear frequently causes me to delay taking action altogether. I tend to delay rather than face failure. However, this anxiety has led me to accept a statement that has completely changed my perspective: failure is not the polar opposite of success; rather, it is an essential part of the path to achieve it.

Here's the thing: failure occurs only when you give up. No matter how many times you fall short, whether it's a lifelong dream or a short-term goal, the act of striving pulls you forward. It is as simple as that. Remember that every step you take, no matter how tiny, represents progress! The trick is to keep moving forward and never lose sight of your goal.

Achieve Your Financial Goals

Whether you're starting a new year, a new month, or simply experiencing the passage of time, don't let fear prevent you from following your financial objectives. Now is the time to dig in and propel yourself forward.

Finally, and most crucially, remember that you only fail if you stop trying. I guarantee that breaking down and implementing your financial goals into digestible bits will make them less enormous, scary, or hairy!

So far in this chapter, we've discussed thinking big and planning smartly. We also discussed several tactics for defining financial goals, the benefits of having financial goals, how to utilize a magic vision board to achieve financial objectives, and how goals can be broken down into smaller chunks for realization.

In the following chapter, I will teach you about the power of financial budgeting, tools and tactics for effective budgeting, and how to use budgeting to improve your financial situation.

Shall we continue?

PART II

Making and Managing Your Dough

Chapter 3

Budgeting: More Than Just Pennies and Dimes

Budgeting is not just for people who do not have enough money. It is for everyone who wants to ensure that their money is enough. – Rosette Mugidde Wamambe

We all have different financial goals that we want to attain in the future, whether it's saving for a comfortable retirement, buying a dream home, or creating wealth. However, to reach these goals and live a stress-free future, you must successfully manage your money. A personal finance budget is one of the most effective financial instruments for assisting you in this process. It serves as a financial road map, allowing you to allocate your money, track your income and expenses, and save for the future.

In this chapter, we'll go over how to start budgeting, what tools you'll need for efficient budget planning, and how budgeting may help you transform your financial life.

So, let us dive deeper!

The Budgeting Basics: Where to Start

A personal budget is a financial plan created to manage income and expenses over a certain period, typically weekly or monthly. It frequently contains a section dedicated to saving money or investing for future goals such as emergencies, education, or retirement.

The fundamental goal of making a personal budget is to effectively manage money, allocate resources sensibly, and meet financial objectives. It is calculated using a variety of parameters, including income, expenses, debts, future aspirations, and so on. Given all of these considerations, a budget enables you to better manage your finances.

Why is Budgeting Important?

We say reduce your dress according to your clothes, which means restricting your expenses based on your income. Budgeting follows this concept by allowing you to manage your costs about your income, making it an essential component of your financial planning. Here are some further reasons why budgeting is a vital tool.

- Budgeting helps manage expenses and prevent overspending.
- Budgeting allows you to set precise financial goals, such as saving for a vacation, buying a home, or paying off debt.
- **Emergency preparedness:** It helps you set aside a certain amount of money for future emergencies.
- **Debt Management:** It helps you track and manage your current debt.
- Budgeting provides peace of mind by managing your finances. Knowing where your money is going and having a plan for the future relieves financial stress and gives you peace of mind.

How to Create a Personal Budget in Six Easy Steps?

A personal finance budget is a financial instrument that allows you to track your spending and save for the future. However, creating a personal budget can be difficult because it requires several processes and judgments. So how can you create a personal budget for yourself?

I'll go over some strategies that will help you create an ideal personal budget and make sound financial decisions.

Find The Objective

It is hard to forecast the future, but a few essential questions must be addressed early in life. For instance, when would you love to retire? What are your plans after you retire? Do you want to buy a home? Whether you desire or have children, and if so, what are your plans for them? List your priorities and write them down. The act of writing them down can help you simplify things, which is referred to as financial planning.

Most people fail to manage their finances because they do not have a clear plan for themselves. This practice will help you determine how much you need to save for each reason and for how long. More significantly, priorities change from time to time, so adjust your financial strategies accordingly.

Identify Your Expenses

Track your family's expenses for two to three months to determine how much is spent on which tasks each month. Identify the absolute need and allocate funds accordingly. First, pay for fixed expenses such as a home loan/rent, a car loan, utility bills, and so on, and then create a budget for variable spending such as grocery shopping, eating out, movie nights, and other activities. Make sure you don't spend more than you've budgeted in each bucket. Also, if you believe you are spending more than you can afford, be sure to analyze your expenses, particularly the variable factors.

Separate Needs from Wants

Separating your needs from your wants is critical for financial independence. We desire many things, but they must be within our budget. Loans and credit cards may appear to provide us with extra purchasing power, but there is always a catch. For example, your car is a depreciating asset, thus it is usually recommended that you buy in a price range that allows you to repay the loan within five years. With simple bank loans, you may buy a $20,000 car when you can only afford one for $8,000, i.e., you can comfortably repay this amount in five years. Given that your earnings and net worth will likely improve over the following five years, you might consider purchasing a $12,000 model for your second automobile. Avoid using credit cards as much as possible. It might devastate the health of your finances.

Plan Ahead

Annual expenses, such as tax, insurance payments, and vacations, can be budgeted. If you set away a tiny amount each month for a certain expense, you will be financially prepared by the end of the year. People frequently take out personal loans for such purposes and continue to pay for them throughout the year, including the interest rate. Simply put, if we can reverse the cycle and plan ahead, we can avoid unnecessary stress and financial loss.

The 50-30-20 rule is one strategy you might apply when planning for the future. This rule assists you in creating a personal budget by dividing your expenses into three categories.

- Allocate 50% of your salary to pay mandatory expenses like rent, phone bills, power, and groceries.
- Set aside 30% of your salary for leisure activities like vacations, shopping, and entertainment.
- Allocate 20% of your salary to savings and investing. You can invest in mutual funds, fixed deposits, PPF, NPS, and other options based on your objectives.

Emergency Corpus

Before you start saving and investing, you should establish an emergency fund. This money is set aside for emergencies; you should never access it unless an emergency arises.

So, how do you define an emergency? Paying your credit card bill is certainly not one of them. This money can help you financially if you lose work, become ill, or have an accident. The amount should cover three to six months' worth of monthly spending. Creating an emergency fund is important to your financial planning and money management.

Make Sure You Save

There is a simple formula for determining how much you can afford to spend.

Income minus Saving = Expenses.

Plan your expenses around this formula. So, how do you determine how much to save?

First, set aside 10% of your income for retirement and never spend it on anything else, even your children's schooling or marriage. Next, determine your future goals and make short-term, mid-term, and long-term strategies based on your priorities. Aside from retirement plans, long-term goals include children's schooling and marriage plans. In contrast, mid-term goals include down payments on a home or automobile, and short-term plans include travel, purchasing gadgets and appliances, etc. Set aside money in each bucket based on your estimate, and use the remainder to construct your budget.

Believe it or not, a little financial discipline can significantly improve the health of your finances. Start modest, but start early, and your money will increase exponentially - this is the best money management guideline.

What Are Some Common Budgeting Mistakes to Avoid?

When we create our budgets, we can all make mistakes. Here are some common budgeting mistakes to avoid for successful financial budgeting.

- Not tracking future expenses, such as vacations, appliance purchases, education, etc. Failure to track these expenses might result in overspending and divergence from the planned budget.
- Neglecting emergency funds which can leave you vulnerable to unanticipated bills.
- Setting unrealistic goals. When creating a budget, aim for feasible goals that align with your income and expenses. It shouldn't be unrealistic.
- Constant monitoring. Budgeting is a continuous process that requires constant monitoring. Failure to adapt your budget can result in a diversion from your overall financial plan.

What Are the Benefits of Maintaining a Personal Budget?

A personal budget is a useful tool to help you navigate your finances more easily. Let's take a look at some of the advantages of maintaining a personal budget:

- Preparing a budget might help you comprehend your financial status.
- Using a budget can help you save for short- and long-term goals.
- Budgeting helps reduce debt by tracking future spending. This allows you to identify and decrease unneeded spending.
- Reduced financial stress. Uncertainty about finances can cause stress and worry. A personal budget provides peace of mind since you know where your money is going and can plan for future expenses.
- Improved decision-making. Budgeting simplifies financial decisions. Before making any purchases or financial obligations, consult your budget to see whether you should proceed.

You've seen how personal finance budgeting can bring financial stability and help you achieve your goals. However, remember that budgeting is not a one-time effort; it requires constant monitoring, and you must be disciplined and consistent with your budget. Sticking to your budget allows you to manage your funds successfully and live a stress-free lifestyle. So, what are you waiting for? Create your personal finance budget and begin your journey to financial freedom.

First, Get These Tools

The idea of proactive money management and budgeting may not appeal to everyone. However, adopting and adhering to a budget are critical first steps toward achieving financial goals, large and small.

Having the right tools is essential for tracking expenditures and monitoring income; fortunately, you don't have to spend a fortune on costly software. Plenty of free apps are available but don't just download the first one you see.

"If you can't keep it (updated), it doesn't get you to the end goal," the goal is to comfortably purchase the things you need while saving for the things you desire, whether that's a fantastic trip or an early retirement.

To assist you in achieving that level of financial freedom, I will provide some simple and free budgeting tools to help you keep your spending under control, ranging from traditional approaches to cutting-edge apps.

Pen & Paper

While budgeting applications and tools are popular, creating a budget requires only a pen and paper.

Using this strategy, basic budgeting entails jotting down all your costs, from monthly payments to tiny discretionary purchases like morning coffee or lunch. Then, categorize those spending as needs or wants. Next, calculate your income. Set aside a portion of your income for necessities first, and any remaining funds can be used for wants.

If your spending exceeds your income, you must decide what changes to make. You may be able to balance your budget by eliminating unnecessary expenses like dining out or a gym subscription. In some circumstances, however, you may need to make more dramatic changes, such as relocating to a lower-cost area.

Expenses OK

The free program Expenses OK simulates the act of budgeting with pen and paper, but the recordkeeping is done digitally.

You have to manually enter every transaction; it is not connected to your bank accounts. Unfortunately, for Android users, the free Expenses OK app is only accessible for iOS devices.

Envelopes

An envelope system involves depositing funds into envelopes labeled for main budget areas such as food, clothing, and dining out. It makes determining how much money is available for each expenditure area simple. When the money in a specific envelope is depleted, it indicates that no further spending should occur in that category until the cash is refilled.

Young, a project manager for the company finance newspaper BizReport, employed this strategy as a college student. It was a strategy his father taught him, and it was easier than navigating the computerized possibilities available 15 years ago. All you have to do is create a list of your monthly financial expenses on an envelope. When your income or money arrives, you select how much you want to spend on each cost and put that money aside in the envelope.

Also, prepare a last envelope for leftovers. After each month, transfer any money left in other envelopes to this envelope to see how much you've saved. The remaining cash in the envelope could then be utilized for any purpose.

Goodbudget

This clever budgeting program is designed for folks who appreciate an envelope cash management method but don't want to deal with the inconvenience of carrying physical envelopes.

"You can make virtual envelopes for your normal expenses, like rent, groceries, or utilities, and fill them with your earnings. Goodbudget is ideal for folks who like a visual and intuitive approach to budgeting and saving. The software will track costs and sync and share budget information across many devices. The free edition offers ten standard envelopes, ten additional envelopes, a year of account history, and access to community help forums.

Spreadsheets

While I tried a free budgeting program in the past, I soon realized it couldn't compete with a spreadsheet. I enjoy being able to modify. My first budgeting spreadsheets were really simple, and I added some features.

I've tried several applications that allow me to enter future costs and expected revenue, but viewing the numbers and a history of income and expenses required a lot of effort. So, I now use an Excel spreadsheet to manage my account. Built-in formulas simplify automating calculations, and spreadsheets can be instantly changed if values change.

Users can create free budget templates with both Microsoft Excel and Google Sheets. Free budget templates are accessible on websites like Life and My Finances and Vertex42. You can also make your own, albeit there may be a learning curve when utilizing the programs. Microsoft's support website offers free online training classes for Office programs. Otherwise, there are lots of tutorials available on YouTube.

Worksheets

If you're creating your first budget, a worksheet can help you avoid guesswork. These documents frequently provide recommended percentages showing how much your earnings should be spent on each category each month.

Many organizations provide free budgeting worksheets online. American Consumer Financial Counseling, a non-profit financial counseling organization, provides sheets for household budgeting, expense tracking, and budgeting for personal needs.

Meanwhile, Regions Bank offers free worksheets for download on its Next Step Financial Education website, including a personal spending plan worksheet and a daily spending tracker.

Banking Tools and Applications

Free budgeting tools could be as close as your bank's website. Bank of America, Chase, and even local credit unions offer budgeting tools that allow clients to track expenses, run spending reports, and export data to spreadsheets or computer applications.

For example, Bank of America's app has an AI-powered virtual assistant named Erica. It assists millions of people in meeting their financial objectives by offering proactive and tailored insights to optimize cash flow, monitor transactions, notify clients of savings possibilities, and more. Meanwhile, the TD Bank app enables customers to create personalized alerts, pay bills automatically, and move funds across accounts. Customers can use the Chase Mobile app's budget tool to manage their monthly spending and see how much money is left after payments and transfers.

MoLO

MoLO, which stands for Money Left Over, is a relatively new app that, unlike many free apps, does not contain advertisements. MoLO offers consumers a simple way to better analyze their expenditures, forecast their monthly cash flow, and detect needless or non-essential spending. Users may connect all their bank accounts to MoLO, automatically tracking their spending, categorizing it, and anticipating how much money they will have left over each month.

SoFi Insights

Another free budgeting app, previously known as SoFi Relay. SoFi Insights enables users to link accounts, examine balances, and establish spending goals. It aggregates accounts and allows you to review expenditures by category easily.

The app also gives users access to VantageScore 3.0 credit scores and makes it easy to connect with a professional to discuss financial objectives and strategies. SoFi Insights subscribers are entitled to a complimentary 30-minute conversation with one of the company's in-house financial counselors. Regardless of which budgeting application you use, I recommend you start tracking your finances immediately. "Don't start tomorrow, start right now."

Know These Tips to Budget Effectively

Budgeting is essential to financial wellness, allowing people to manage their money sensibly, save for the future, and achieve their financial objectives. Effective budgeting skills are vital for paying off debt, saving for a significant purchase, or building an emergency fund. Let's look at some practical budgeting tactics and financial ideas to help you gain control of your finances.

Create a Realistic Budget

Create a realistic budget that includes your income, expenses, and financial goals. Track your monthly income and expenses, separating fixed (mortgage, utilities) and variable (entertainment, dining out) costs. Make sure your budget matches your financial priorities and lifestyle.

Set Clear Financial Goals

Set short- and long-term financial goals to help guide your budgeting efforts. Defining quantifiable goals for vacation savings, emergency fund building, or student loan repayment provides focus and drive. Break down larger goals into manageable chunks to track your progress more efficiently.

Differentiate Between Needs and Wants

When making budget allocations, distinguish between critical necessities and discretionary wants. Prioritize basic needs like shelter, utilities, and groceries. While discretionary spending on leisure and non-essential things can be fun, keeping balance is critical for staying within budget.

Use The 50/30/20 Rule

The 50/30/20 rule is a popular budgeting guideline that recommends allocating 50% of income to needs, 30% to discretionary spending, and 20% to savings and debt reduction. Adjust these percentages to suit your financial objectives and circumstances, but the principle highlights the significance of balancing consumption and saving.

Emergency Fund

Creating an emergency fund is essential to having sound financial standing. Set up three to six months' living expenses to handle unexpected situations such as medical bills, auto repairs, or job loss. Having an emergency reserve prevents you from relying on credit cards or loans in unexpected circumstances.

**Automate Savings
and Debt Payments**

Automating savings and debt payments guarantees that you reach your financial goals consistently. Set up automated transfers to your savings account and set aside funds for debt repayment to avoid the temptation of discretionary spending.

**Review And
Adjust Regularly**

A successful budget is dynamic and flexible. Regularly examine your budget to determine its effectiveness and alter categories as needed. Life events, income fluctuations, and shifting financial goals may need changes to your budgeting technique.

Negotiate Bills and Expenses

Take aggressive actions to lower fixed costs by negotiating bills and looking for better service bargains. Contact your service providers for discounts, or consider switching to lower-cost alternatives. Small modifications might add up to big savings over time.

Avoid Impulse Purchases

Impulse purchases can disrupt your budgetary efforts. Create shopping lists, compare costs, and give yourself time to think about non-essential purchases to help you spend less. Delaying gratification frequently leads to more deliberate spending.

Invest In Financial Education

Continuous learning about personal finance improves your ability to make sound financial decisions. Spend time educating yourself on investing possibilities, retirement planning, and debt control. Knowledge helps you manage the financial landscape more efficiently.

Effective budgeting is more than just limiting expenditure; it's a dynamic tool that may help you reach financial freedom and stability. Setting clear goals, distinguishing between necessities and wants, and adopting proactive financial practices will help you master your money and provide the groundwork for long-term financial success. Remember, good budgeting is an ongoing process that evolves along your financial journey, so stay dedicated and modify as needed to attain your financial goals.

Transitioning From Scarcity to Abundance

The awareness that there are sufficient resources for everyone is the essence of the abundant mindset. Even while that sounds good, it's hard to think everyone has access to an ample supply of opportunity, money, food, and other necessities. As a result, it's simple to acquire the opposite perspective, known as the scarcity mindset, which holds that resources are limited. When you have a scarcity attitude, giving others who helped with the production credit and recognition or profit and power is hard. Genuinely celebrating the accomplishments of others might be difficult when you have a scarcity attitude. Because your mentality greatly influences your perspective of the world. Let's examine each one in more detail. Scarcity Mindset: When you believe that there are only a finite number of resources in the world, you become pessimistic and self-centered. You may, therefore, hold the following opinions as a result of your:

- Find it difficult to acknowledge, thank, and praise other people.
- Find it difficult to consider win-win scenarios.
- Prioritize your interests over other people's.
- Find it difficult to feel joy for other people's accomplishments.

As you can see, these views are egotistical and lack appeal to other people. The zero-sum mentality, which holds that for you to succeed, someone else must lose, is the foundation of the scarcity mindset. You do your hardest to acquire the largest piece since you believe there isn't enough pie for everyone. In actuality, though, there is enough for everyone. You can win even if the other person loses.

Potential Effects of a Scarcity Mindset on You

You can understand what it's like to make decisions with a scarcity mindset if you've ever made a snap decision because you didn't have enough time to consider all possible outcomes.

This is because our thoughts can only handle a certain amount of data simultaneously. Having to constantly plan to outsmart consumes bandwidth and impairs cognitive function, which might result in counterproductive acts.

When you function at this lower cognitive level, you may make decisions that seem (or might even be!) uncontrollable at the time but are ultimately counterproductive. Among them are:

- Receiving preventative care less frequently
- Not taking prescription drugs as directed
- Generally having a lower tendency to keep appointments
- Not producing as much at work or home
- Unable to provide careful parenting
- Choosing unwise financial decisions

Your prefrontal cortex, the part of the brain linked to making decisions, becomes less active when you're mentally exhausted, much like when a computer tries to execute too many programs simultaneously. Making decisions requires a longer response time, increased stress, and decreased confidence. Planning gets too difficult.

Furthermore, greater scarcity can influence one's perspective and thinking. Our collective capacity for rapid decision-making has declined due to catastrophes such as the 2008 financial crisis (and perhaps also during the coronavirus pandemic and the ensuing economic anxiety).

Developing an Attitude of Abundance

Dopamine is released into our brains when we take risks and come out on top of them; this primes our brains to look for more dopamine by boosting the growth behaviors that first triggered the dopamine release.

Acceptance

A component of the development mentality is the desire to move forward in life. —but accepting it is helpful to proceed. By doing this, you give up trying to force yourself to accept where you are right now with your limited and priceless resources. You must know where you've come from to know where you're heading.

Self-Empathy

You should be proud of yourself for surviving to this day because everything you have done in your life up to this point has brought you here. Every behavior or attitude you wish to change today once had a function or purpose—survival. Practice self-compassion.

Locate That One Thing

You may not have much money, but you have much spare time. Consider that a valuable area of abundance in your life. Or perhaps you are financially prosperous but so busy earning your money that you don't have much time for yourself. You realize that even though you wish to spend more time with your family, they benefit from your abundance.

Not a lot of money or time on your hands? Perhaps you are surrounded by affection, whether from a person or a pet. Even if it's simply that you're alive today, there's probably at least one thing in your life that you may consider bountiful.

Define What Abundance Means to You

Everybody sees abundance and a rich attitude in different ways. For someone else, what is abundant to you may appear scarce, and vice versa. Adopting an abundant mindset might be challenging if you don't know what you're aiming for. What would it feel like to have plenty? How would you describe your life?

Start Small

Making drastic changes to your routines or ways of thinking at once—in any field—may lead to irrational expectations in yourself. Which aspect of your life do you think your scarcity mentality most impeded?

Start by making minor adjustments to your perspective there. Do you find it difficult to find time these days? Consider the activities you enjoy with your time or what you could provide.

Being Mindful

It makes sense that the scarcity attitude would ingrain itself into our thinking. They are always thinking about what they should do to stay alive. This removes us from the here and now. Our brains can be slowed down to enable clearer thinking by setting aside time to practice mindfulness, whether through meditation or simply focusing on the here and now.

Writing in a Journal

Journaling can be helpful if you are having trouble defining abundance for yourself. It can help you pinpoint areas where you are abundant now and places where you would like to concentrate on becoming more affluent.

Eliminating Debt Professionally

America's household debt total is $16.15 trillion. Therefore, you're not alone if you're feeling the burden of debt from credit cards, auto loans, school loans, and other sources. Debt is commonplace.

But you're being held back by this normal. You can't save for the future when you always pay for the past. Furthermore, debt is making every month far too tight, with inflation at an all-time high.

I'm happy to inform you that you are no longer required to be normal. You don't have to be included in the $16.15 trillion estimate. You may stop squandering this month's income on last months or last year's expenditures by learning how to pay off debt. You can reclaim your money!

Let's see how to accomplish it and let's look into it:

Methods for Paying Off Debt

Let's start by defining debt. This is the basic definition of debt: any amount of money owed to anyone, for any reason, is considered debt. With that framework in place, let's discuss eliminating debt from your life. Forever and ever more.

Determine Your Debt Level

Consider it this way. You can't climb a mountain if you don't know how huge it is. Furthermore, if you avoid giants, you cannot defeat them. That is similar to what Socrates said, isn't it? Not at all? Still, it's sound advice. You must acknowledge the full amount of your debt if you wish to pay it off. But pay attention—this is the beginning of the win, not the point of failure! You can pay off your debt. You also will.

However, you must first determine the amount of debt you must pay off. Look up and record the total amount of all your debts.

Establish A Budget

All budget is a financial plan. It's how you direct every dollar, so you don't have to worry where they've all disappeared. You don't have time for misplaced money right now. You have a job lined up for that money because you are paying off debt.

Make a budget, then. Now! Ensure your budget accounts for your debt-paying objective, cover all the necessities, and give up certain frills (even temporarily) to free up more money for debt repayment.

Apply the Debt Snowball Method

Now that your spending plan is established, it's time to begin debt repayment! And using the debt snowball method is the most effective way to achieve precisely that. Since you're paying off your bills from smallest to greatest, it's how you gain momentum.

Yes, that is accurate. Begin with the least amount of debt you can.

We know that many individuals advocate paying off your biggest debt—or the one with the highest interest rate—first. On the surface, the math sounds reasonable, but if we were using math, we wouldn't have taken on debt in the first place. Furthermore, eliminating debt involves more than simply math. It concerns altering behavior.

The debt snowball method can help you see immediate results and feel like you're making progress if your goal is to eliminate debt.

How Credit Snowballs Works

- Do you still have the list of debts you wrote down? Ignore the interest rates and arrange them from the least to the largest.
- Pay the minimal amount owed on every loan, excluding the smallest one. Use all the additional cash you have to take that one on. This encompasses the funds you liberated during the budgetary process.
- After paying off the smallest obligation, apply that payment (together with any remaining funds) to the next-smallest loan and pay it off.
- Keep going until all bills are settled.

The amount you're paying on your debt increases in size and momentum with each loan you pay off, much like a snowball rolling down a hill.

Stop Using Debt

If you keep digging, you will never be able to escape a hole. You break up with debt when you choose to pay it off. Permanently. Put an end to credit card swipes. Same-as-cash frauds are over. Financing luxury autos is over.

Paying off debt with all your might will just serves to compound your debt. Leave the hole. Inhale the clean breath of liberty. And never turn around again.

Types of Debt

Alright, let me discuss the four primary categories of debt to shed some light on this subject:

- Secured debt refers to loans, such as auto loans, secured by collateral.
- Unlike credit cards, unsecured debt lacks collateral.
- A credit card or home equity line of credit is an example of revolving debt.
- A one-time lump sum loan is a nonrevolving debt (e.g., a mortgage, auto financing, school loans).

Furthermore, there are other methods to incur debt, including:

- Student loans
- Auto loans

- Bank cards
- Debt from medical expenses
- Loans secured by home equity
- Payday advances
- Individual loans
- Government debt and the IRS

Remember, too, that deceptive debt includes things like buy now, pay later installment programs. While these may seem like a fantastic idea at the time, they are a definite method to add to the $16.15 trillion total debt the United States currently possesses.

How to Repay Debt

Thus, it is true that there are numerous methods to accrue debt. Furthermore, there are numerous approaches to debt relief. Some are truly useful, while others are not. Just being truthful.

Consolidation of Debt

One method of combining several debts into a single payment is debt consolidation. At first, it seems like a smart plan, but then you realize that your loans have longer terms, which means you'll be in debt for longer.

And guess what? That low interest rate seems so enticing right now. It typically increases with time as well.

In summary, paying off debt over a longer period while accruing interest is not a good deal. Thus, this approach is not recommended.

Avalanche of Debt

When you pay off your debt from the greatest to the lowest interest rate, regardless of balance, you commit the debt avalanche, also known as debt stacking. Initially, the math appears to be perfect. However, our innate wiring is the issue rather than the mathematics.

Repaying debt is challenging. A speedy victory spurs you on and keeps you going. When you have a mountain of debt, and it takes a long time to pay it off, your motivation can go out faster than a wildfire in the rain.

Debt Reduction

Companies that settle debts are the murky underbelly of the financial industry. Steer clear of this choice. Businesses will take your money and then guarantee to bargain with your creditors to lower your debt. Typically, they simply take your money and absolve you of any debt. Hard pass, huh?

Borrowing Money to Pay Off Debt

It seems absurd to read that title by itself. Why would you take on more debt if you were paying off debt?

That directly relates to our previous discussion about pulling oneself out of a hole. It. Does not. Work. Furthermore, the dirt is more difficult to remove the deeper you go. You eventually find yourself submerged. Nevertheless, there are many scams out there that attempt to convince you to do it. They try to sell you on the idea that you're a savvy consumer who can take advantage of your retirement savings or the equity in your house (for a HELOC) to your benefit, or they might persuade you to apply for a new credit card to pay off your existing ones.

Some of these techniques produce a brief debt relief. Put the word "temporary" in emphasis. The issue only gets worse. Instead of paying off debt, you're positioning yourself for a massive debt accumulation.

Ultimately, these kinds of debt relief programs cannot assist you in resolving the underlying problem that brought you here in the first place.

You don't have to borrow, settle, or consolidate money to pay off your debt. It's simple: You need to adjust how you manage your finances. You must settle your loan.

The Debt Snowball Is the Best Method for Paying Off Debt

The debt snowball method is one that we have already discussed, but since it is the only strategy that truly reduces debt, we must include it in our list of debt repayment strategies.

By using the debt snowball method, you avoid escalating your debt, borrowing against your future or your assets, lengthening the duration of your loans, raising interest rates, and diminishing your motivation. You also avoid clinging to a short-term solution that will only make things worse down the road.

You're adjusting your financial situation as necessary to ultimately succeed. One loan at a time, you are concentrating on and paying off your obligations. You're gaining inspiration and the extra push you need to press on.

You are regaining control over your income by permanently ignoring your loan payments.

Advice on How to Reduce Debt More Quickly

You're prepared to pay off debt, (Wow, this is big.) Now, you need some pointers to help you get there more quickly.

Pay Off Debt Before Investing in Retirement

We'll start by addressing the two major obstacles in any debt repayment process. The first is trying to focus too much of your energy on multiple financial goals at once. The most common reason for this is when someone wants to pay off debt and put money toward retirement at the same time.

Progress is slowed down, to start. It also indicates that you aren't focusing on your debt-reduction approach.

You see, your income is the most powerful instrument you have to develop wealth. Furthermore, your debt is robbing you. Stealing from the future to make up for the past. Obtain. It. Vanished.

Take full advantage of it. After it's gone, put money aside for a fully-funded emergency fund so that debt won't ever be an attraction or a justification.

Next, begin your retirement savings. This strategy works. Your best bet is to pay off your debt before saving for the future. You may pursue your investing objectives after you regain control over your entire income.

Stop Using Credit Cards

The second major obstacle to being debt-free is credit cards. Now, you may think that debt isn't necessarily associated with credit cards. as you always repay them. Am I correct?

However, consider this: why would you have the option to return to debt in your pocket if your goal is to permanently eliminate it?

Would you carry a candy bar in your backpack if you were attempting to break your sugar habit? Debt is also a habit. Recall that to get out of debt and stay out of it, you must alter your behavior. Furthermore, having easy access to tools that facilitate reverting to your previous behavior is not a good idea.

Pay off more than simply your credit card debt. Put an end to the temptation. Give up using credit cards and start living without them.

Lower Your Expenses

In the second stage of using the debt snowball strategy, I advised throwing all your surplus money at the smallest bill. There are two excellent ways to earn that "extra money."

The first step is to reduce your spending.

This may appear to be lowering any budget lines that you can. If you're used to buying new clothes every month, reduce your budget to only the necessities, such as new jeans for the child growing two inches.

Another strategy to save money is eliminating certain costs from your budget. Become your barista. Stop paying for an ad-free version of your favorite music streaming service. Begin preparing your meals and stop eating out for now.

That is the key for now. This is a time to give up certain things to obtain something amazing: liberation from debt.

Increase Your Income

You can also acquire extra money by increasing your income. Start a side hustle, work extra hours, request a raise, change employment, freelance, or sell items.

You know you have things lying around the house that you no longer use. Is any of this worth money? You may be surprised! You can declutter your life and save money to pay off your debt. That is a win-win situation.

Yes, all of these solutions need time and effort—but the more you implement immediately, the faster you'll be debt-free!

Do Not Give Up

You may have reasons why now is not the time to address your debt. However, there will always be excuses to put this off. So don't. Also, once you get started, be prepared for life to throw up unexpected roadblocks that make sticking to your plan difficult.

But hear this: It is still possible. If something knocks you off the debt-payoff route, get back up, regain your feet, and get back on track.

Let's discuss a few practical issues you may encounter now or in the future.

Income: Even if you have a poor salary or live on one income, you can pay off your debt. Use those strategies to cut costs inc, increase your revenue, and be patient. Your trip may take a little longer, but you will be debt-free. You. Will.

Inflation: Inflation is another issue that is now draining people's budgets. You may believe you are running out of money, but growing expenditures will not prevent you from eliminating your debt. Get into that budget and start making changes. Again, it will not be easy. But you can do it.

Motivation: What do you do when you lose your motivation? First, realize you are not alone. It's extremely normal to begin a goal enthusiastically but then lose steam as you progress.

But do not give up! You are in charge of this financial goal. Remind yourself of your why. What is the payoff for all of this effort?

- Feeling confident and in charge of your finances?
- How can we stop comparing ourselves and instead achieve contentment?
- Preparing your children for a financially secure future through ownership rather than owing?

All of this comes with a debt-free lifestyle. And all of that awaits you on the other side of this adventure. Yes, debt is the norm. Disrupt the norm. Pay off your debts. Every last dime. No matter your income. Regardless of your past. You can shape your future.

Developing The Habit of Saving

Saving money is an important skill that protects our financial future and gives us a sense of stability and empowerment. Cultivating a habit of saving requires a combination of mentality, techniques, and persistent actions. This section discusses numerous ways and strategies for developing a strong saving habit.

First and foremost, it is critical to set a clear purpose. A stated goal, whether for an emergency fund, a specific purchase, retirement, or an investment, gives you focus and incentive. With a clear goal, you may develop a realistic savings strategy by breaking down the larger goal into smaller, more doable tasks.

Second, developing the appropriate mentality is critical. Recognizing the importance of delayed gratification is critical in saving money. Understanding that making short-term sacrifices can lead to long-term financial security is an effective motivation. Changing your attitude to see saving as a pleasant habit rather than a limiting practice can greatly impact one's willingness to save.

A budget is vital for developing the habit of saving. A budget acts as a road map for managing spending and identifying areas where savings might be increased. Tracking income and costs allows you to find areas where you may cut back on discretionary spending and dedicate more money to savings.

Automating savings is an effective method. Setting up recurring transfers from a checking account to a savings account ensures that a percentage of your salary is constantly saved before being spent. This strategy removes the incentive to spend money originally intended for savings.

Furthermore, adopting economical habits can considerably increase savings. Simple actions such as meal planning, lowering energy use, avoiding impulse purchases, and seeking discounts or using coupons can result in significant long-term savings. These seemingly modest tweaks can greatly influence your overall financial health.

Furthermore, it is critical to educate oneself about personal finance continually. Understanding investment fundamentals, compound interest, and numerous saving methods can help people make better financial decisions. This knowledge can assist you in identifying possibilities to expand your funds successfully.

Another effective method is to surround oneself with a supportive community. Sharing your experiences and insights with like-minded people and seeking direction from financial experts and mentors can provide encouragement, counsel, and accountability as you work to create a saving habit.

Finally, it is critical to acknowledge and celebrate accomplishments and development. Acknowledging and praising oneself for meeting savings goals, no matter how small reinforces the habit and offers encouragement to continue saving.

Remember that creating a habit of saving money is a slow and ongoing process that takes dedication, discipline, and the proper mindset. Individuals can achieve financial security and peace of mind by defining clear goals, cultivating a saving mindset, creating a budget, automating saves, adopting thrifty habits, educating themselves, requesting help, and celebrating accomplishments.

Remember that tiny measures taken today might lead to tremendous progress tomorrow.

Chapter 4
Growing Your Cash Stash

"Try to save something while your salary is small; it's impossible to save after you begin to earn more" -Jack Benny

You've read many money-management books, but how many of them sound fun? Indeed, far too many of them present mind-boggling figures and concepts that typically include self-deprivation and claim to finally lead to that dream home or retirement at the age of 60.

The good news is that there is a more straightforward method to develop your stash—no need to slog through difficult statistics or burrow down and deny yourself fundamental pleasures.

Simple modifications to your mentality and lifestyle can still help you save money. So, in this chapter, I'll provide suggestions and cheat sheets on how to expand your money, as well as some hidden tactics for financial success.

Shall we proceed?

Strategies for Financial Growth

If you don't plan, you plan to fail. This may sound like an old cliché, but it highlights an essential component of personal finance. Financial planning can be scary, but it does not have to be. There are a few basic ways to get your money in order and improve your financial status. Whether you're struggling with debt or want to save more money, these tactics can help you achieve your financial objectives. Let's dive right in.

Define Your Financial Goals

Financial planning is an essential component of leading a secure and fulfilling life. The first step in developing a sound financial plan is identifying your objectives. These can include long-term plans like debt repayment or setting up a college fund for your offspring, as well as short-term ones like saving for a vacation or a car. Creating realistic objectives is critical, so break them down into smaller chunks and set attainable benchmarks to keep you motivated.

When you've identified objectives that are meaningful to you, you may construct a budget outlining how and when these objectives will be reached. Remember not to overextend yourself when budgeting and planning—stay within your means. Don't bite more than you can chew. Breaking financial goals into smaller, more manageable portions can provide visible evidence of accomplishment while boosting morale and motivating even greater efforts toward future success.

Track Your Spending and Income

Managing your funds is not difficult if you follow a structured method. Tracking your expenses and income is an important aspect of financial management. It is critical to track every cent that enters and exits your accounts, whether from an annual wage, a side venture, or incurred expenses such as rent, bills, etc. This will not only help you avoid going over budget on purchases but also give you vital insights into where you may make better financial decisions in the future. Numerous online solutions are available to make tracking quicker and more convenient for everyone.

Create a Budget

Creating a budget for yourself might be an excellent method to establish a financial strategy. Knowing how much money comes in and goes out each month can allow you to better manage your finances. Setting up a budget takes time and effort, but having one in place can provide peace of mind, knowing your finances are in order and your accounts are functioning smoothly. To begin, compile a list of all your income sources, including your work and other investments.

Then, calculate how much money will be required for certain expenses such as food, utilities, loan payments, and other bills so that you can save or spend each month. Furthermore, you should consider creating actionable categories with associated goals, such as paying off debt or investing for retirement, so that these targets seem attainable rather than distant dreams. A well-crafted budget is necessary to develop solid financial habits and achieve long-term success.

Invest in Yourself: Take Courses and Learn About Financial Planning

Investing in yourself is among the most essential decisions you can make. Taking personal finance and financial planning classes can help you learn how to manage your money, prioritize savings, decrease debt, increase investments, and plan for retirement. Learning the fundamentals of budgeting, debt management, and investing will enable you to create strong financial strategies that will serve you well throughout your life.

Taking a personal finance course provides advice on the steps needed to protect one's financial future. Understandably, these courses provide skills and information that will enable you to make the most effective use of your resources and make informed financial decisions.

Maintain Financial Discipline

Maintaining financial discipline is critical for ensuring your future stability. To accomplish this, I recommend assessing your present financial status and developing a budget that works for you. This budget should include all your expenses, such as utility bills and living expenses, so you can get a clear picture of your monthly spending.

Once this is developed, you can revisit it regularly to find new ways to save money or generate more income. It's also critical to monitor or maintain track of any investments you make, regardless of size, and to stay current on any changes or new developments in the globe or economy that may impact your investing strategy. No matter how little the investment, you must exercise caution and discipline in all aspects of your finances.

Maintaining an emergency fund to handle unforeseen expenses.

Having money set up for unexpected expenses that may come throughout your life is critical. An emergency fund can help you pay for these costs without putting you in financial trouble. Having a certain amount of accessible cash can keep you from taking out loans or using credit cards to meet unexpected expenses. It is critical to prepare and select how much you want to put into this fund and what constitutes an "emergency" expense. With a plan in place, it will be easier to save the necessary finances and have peace of mind if a financial emergency arises.

Everyone's financial journey is unique, but some common themes regarding financial success exist. Define your goals, track your progress, create a budget, and invest in yourself—if you do all these things, you'll be on your road to a prosperous financial future. Maintain discipline, and don't let unexpected expenses put you off track.

Diversifying Revenue Streams

Visualize yourself as an orchestra conductor. You're standing on a podium before a sea of great musicians. Each musician carries a different instrument. You wave your baton, and a symphony of harmonizing sounds reverberates around the hall. Imagine these instruments as your numerous revenue streams.

Diversifying your income streams is similar to generating harmonized symphonic music. It improves the resilience and growth potential of your business. You transform into a lovely tune of financial prosperity.

Diversified income streams are multiple sources of earnings that contribute to your finances. They are your orchestra's unique instruments. Each one adds to the overall performance and generates a harmonic income balance.

So, why is diversifying revenue streams necessary for financial mastery? Let's have a look into this.

Understanding Income Diversification

Before we get into the practical methods, let's first understand the importance of income diversification. Consider a garden with a variety of plants. Each plant has its own set of characteristics that contribute to the ecosystem's general health, attractiveness, and durability. The flowers' brilliant colors attract pollinators, and the big trees provide shade and protection for lesser plants and animals. Similarly, diversifying your income entails creating multiple revenue streams, each with unique strengths and benefits. This method not only reduces risk but also increases your financial well-being.

You may build a strong and durable financial foundation when you have numerous revenue streams. Diversifying your income acts as a protective barrier, similar to how a well-balanced environment preserves stability through the interaction of different species. When one source of income fails, another can cover the gap. Like a flock of birds flying in a "V" formation, each bird takes turns leading the way, providing a clear path ahead. Diversifying reduces the impact of uncertainties like job loss, economic downturns, and unexpected expenses.

The Importance of Diversifying Your Income

Income diversification is not a luxury but a need in today's fast-changing environment. The old idea of relying entirely on one profession or source of money is becoming more dangerous. Industries can rise and fall quickly with technical breakthroughs and changing market circumstances. Diversifying your income allows you to adjust to this new reality while setting yourself up for long-term success.

Furthermore, income diversification enables you to pursue new chances and broaden your horizons. It inspires you to leave your comfort zone and discover hidden abilities or passions. Each revenue stream, like a garden with various plants, presents its own set of problems and benefits. This variety keeps you engaged, motivated, and always learning.

Fundamental Principles of Income Diversification

Now, let's look at the fundamental ideas of income diversification and the components that make this plan effective. I would encourage you to consider it a formula for financial resiliency.

- **Spread the Risk:** Rather than relying on a single source of income, diversify your interests over several domains. In this manner, if one industry or area suffers, others can help balance things. For example, if you work full-time, consider investing in stocks, real estate or launching a side business. This diversity ensures that your financial well-being is not exclusively determined by the success or failure of one venture.

- **Capitalizing on Your Strengths:** Determine your particular abilities and hobbies, then investigate matching revenue streams. By doing what you enjoy, work becomes less of a struggle and more of a wonderful journey. For example, if you have writing skills, you can work as a freelance content writer, start a blog, or even write and publish a book. In this manner, you can diversify your income and enjoy the process.

- **Budgeting and Saving:** Manage your finances properly by setting aside a percentage of your salary and planning for unexpected gaps or emergencies. This practice enables you to create a safety net and remain stable during your journey. With a strong financial foundation, you can confidently pursue new income prospects without worrying about going into debt or experiencing financial trouble.

Remember that income diversification isn't a one-size-fits-all solution. It takes careful analysis of your situation, risk tolerance, and long-term objectives. By following these basic concepts, you may build a diversified income strategy that protects your financial future and opens up new opportunities and fulfillment.

Steps for Diversifying Your Income

Now that you've learned about the necessity and concepts of income diversification let's get down to business and look at how to implement them.

Diversifying your income is similar to creating a garden with various fruits and veggies. Each revenue source functions like a distinct plant, contributing to your financial environment's overall abundance and stability. You may build a strong and profitable financial future by discovering and developing these income streams.

Identifying Potential Income Streams

Begin your journey by identifying prospective revenue streams. Like a treasure hunt, this method entails looking for hidden jewels matching your abilities and hobbies. Seek revenue-generating options in addition to your principal income source.

Consider freelancing, creating your own business, or investing in stocks or real estate. Freelancing allows you to use your talents and knowledge to give client services on a flexible schedule. Starting a side business allows you to turn your passion into a profit, whether you sell handmade items or provide specialized consulting services. Investing in equities or real estate can result in passive income and long-term growth.

Remember that each revenue stream should supplement your present talents and lifestyle. Consider what you enjoy and are skilled at. This will ensure that you earn money and discover meaning in the process.

Dealing with Financial Uncertainty

Diversifying your income might create new risks, particularly in the beginning. A good financial strategy that provides for unexpected circumstances is essential. As a mountain climber gets ready for shifting weather, stockpile supplies to withstand unforeseen tempests. Create an emergency fund, make sure you have enough insurance, and stick to a reasonable spending plan to help you through any financial turbulence.

Managing Time and Energy Across Several Revenue Sources

It takes careful time management and prioritization to manage many revenue streams. Strike a balance that will help you manage your time like juggling with several balls in the air. Arrange and plan your work so that every source of revenue gets the time and attention it needs. Adopt productivity tools and strategies to reduce workload and prevent burnout.

Keep in mind that there isn't a one-size-fits-all strategy as you set out on the path of income diversification. Since every person's circumstance and objective are different, you must adjust your plan accordingly. You can lay a strong basis for future success and financial security by making risky decisions, growing your revenue streams, and adjusting to shifting circumstances.

Investing Wisely for Future Wealth

If you've never invested before, you might want to run away from the idea of forking over your money in the hopes that it will either multiply or not. Indeed, investing will always carry some risk, but it also can increase your money with little effort and give you additional income to help you reach your financial objectives. It involves more than just putting money into investments; it also involves making wise investments. Numerous strategies exist for making wise investments; some are quite effective, while others result in financial ruin. I'll go over a few things with you here that you should think about before you invest your money.

Create a Financial Roadmap for Yourself

If you haven't created a financial plan before, take some time to sit down and honestly assess your current financial status before making any investment decisions. Determining your objectives and risk tolerance, either on your own or with the assistance of a financial expert, is the first step toward smart investing. Your ability to profit from your investments is not guaranteed. However, you should be able to achieve financial security over time and reap the rewards of money management if you learn the truth about investing and saving and carry out a wise strategy.

Determine How Comfortable You Are Taking Risks

Every investment has some level of risk. You should be aware that investing in securities like stocks, bonds, or mutual funds carries a risk of losing all or part of your money. Your principal—the money you initially invested—could be lost. That remains valid even if you buy your investments from a bank.

Posing a bigger investment return is the benefit of taking on risk. If your financial objective is long-term, you will probably generate more money if you carefully invest in riskier asset classes like stocks or bonds as opposed to limiting your portfolio to safer options like cash equivalents. For short-term financial objectives, however, investing only in cash may be appropriate. For investors in cash equivalents, inflation risk—the possibility that inflation could eventually outstrip profits and reduce them—is the main source of concern.

Think About a Suitable Combination of Investments

An investor may contribute to protection against substantial losses by including asset classes in their portfolio that have investment returns that fluctuate depending on the state of the market. Historically, the returns of the three primary asset classes—stocks, bonds, and cash—have not changed at the same time. When market conditions favor one asset class, other asset classes typically receive average or mediocre returns. You can lower your chance of losing money and improve the total investment returns on your portfolio by investing in multiple asset classes. You will be able to offset your losses in one asset category with higher investment returns in another asset category if the return on your investments in one asset category declines.

Furthermore, asset allocation is crucial since it significantly affects your chances of achieving your financial objectives. Your investments could not yield a high enough return to reach your objective if you don't take on enough risk in your portfolio. For example, most financial experts concur that you will probably need to incorporate at least some stock or stock mutual funds in your portfolio if you are saving for a long-term goal, like retirement or college.

When making large investments in employer stock or any other type of stock, use caution.

Diversifying your investments is one of the most crucial strategies to reduce the risks associated with investing. It is logical to spread your assets over several accounts. Within an asset class, you might be able to minimize losses and lessen return variations on your investments by selecting the appropriate group of investments without giving up too much potential gain.

If you make large investments in shares of your employer's stock, or any other stock, you run a serious risk of losing money on your investments. You will almost definitely lose a lot of money (and possibly your job) if that stock performs poorly or the company files for bankruptcy.

Establish and Keep an Emergency Fund

Most wise investors have enough cash in their savings products to cover unforeseen costs, such as an unexpected job loss. Some people make sure they save up to half of their salary each month so they know they will have it when they need it.

Pay Off Credit Card Debt with A High Interest Rate

There isn't a single investing option out there that pays off as well as paying off all of your high-interest debt while posing less risk. The best course of action, regardless of the state of the market, if you have debt from high-interest credit cards is to pay off the entire amount as soon as possible.

Take a Look at Dollar Cost Averaging

By using the investment method known as "dollar cost averaging," which involves consistently adding new money to your investment over an extended period, you can guard against the risk of investing all your money at the wrong time. You will purchase more assets at cheap prices and fewer at high prices if you consistently make the same amount of money into your investments. Especially in a volatile market, individuals who typically make a lump-sum contribution to an IRA at the end of the year or in early April may wish to consider "dollar cost averaging" as an investment strategy.

Make Use of Your Employer's "Free Money"

Your employer may match all or part of your contributions in many employer-sponsored retirement plans. You are losing out on "free money" for your retirement savings if your workplace has a retirement plan and you don't contribute enough to receive the full match.

Think About Periodically Rebalancing Your Portfolio

Returning your portfolio to its initial asset allocation mix is known as rebalancing. By rebalancing, you may make sure that none of the asset classes in your portfolio are overemphasized and bring it back to a risk level that is comfortable for you.

To rebalance your portfolio, you can use your investments or the calendar. Rebalancing an investor's portfolio regularly, say every six or twelve months, is advised by many financial gurus. The benefit of this approach is that the calendar serves as a helpful reminder of when to think about rebalancing. Others advise against rebalancing until an asset class's relative weight shifts by more than a predetermined percentage. This strategy has the benefit of having your investments tell you when it's time to rebalance. In either scenario, rebalancing functions best when it is done seldom.

Steer Clear of Situations That Could Lead to Fraud

Scammers also peruse blog and newspaper headlines. They frequently exploit a widely reported news story to entice possible investors and give their "opportunity" a more authentic appearance. Before investing, the SEC advises you to research the answers to your questions from a reliable source. Before investing, always take your time and consult with family and friends you can trust.

Investing can help you achieve some of your bigger, more expensive financial objectives and position yourself for future financial stability. To make sure that your portfolio is by your most important financial objectives, take the time to analyze your budget to ascertain how much you can afford to invest. You should also carefully consider your timeframe and risk tolerance when choosing which investments to make.

Being frugal without Being Stingy

I'd like to start by posing an unusual query to you. Have you ever become sick and sought medical advice from a doctor? If so, I'm very certain you've taken some of the medication that the doctor prescribed. Even while using medication to recover may not seem pleasant at the moment, it is essential to get better. After your sickness has passed, you express gratitude to the doctor for recommending the appropriate medications for you. The same holds for cost-cutting.

At first, you might find it difficult to save money, and you might not even find the concept appealing. However, you soon understand the value of saving when you experience its advantages.

Yes, being frugal does not mean being a miser.

One thing is certain: to live a rich life, one must save money. Sometimes you need money to achieve your goals in life. A fancy car, a trip to your dream holiday spot, a home purchase, and a post-retirement life are all financial obligations. They don't just show up. And you must unavoidably save money to do that.

Let me give an example to help you understand this. Assume Andrews recently announced his retirement from the military. He had never bothered to save money during his working years, believing that only misers do so. He used to squander every penny he made without setting aside any money. He didn't care about conserving money; he lived life on his terms.

However, he no longer has a source of income and no money to sustain his retired lifestyle.

Just picture the kind of life he will lead in the future. Could he carry on with his way of life and his standard of living? Could he have a prosperous and contented retirement?

Without a doubt. He would not be able to continue living at his previous level.

All of this occurred simply as a result of his lack of savings.

Andrews would still be living a contented life, financially independent, and, of course, extremely wealthy if he had saved money.

So, do you still think that misers should be the ones who save money? Don't allow this to occur to you. Also, once you begin saving, the act of saving itself will start to seem like an exciting endeavor rather than a miserly one. Additionally, saving money doesn't require being a miser; it's not at all difficult.

Allow me to demonstrate

You may start saving money every day. Let's keep this sum modest. Not an issue. Here, the practice of saving money should be emphasized. Make it a point to keep a piggy bank filled with any spare change at the end of the day. And remember to save every day. This modest sum will motivate you to save more.

After that, you may start creating your monthly budget by listing all of the places, amounts, and savings you would like to achieve. It is possible to save money while still having a fulfilling life. Smaller measures like cutting back on your monthly grocery spending, dining out costs, shopping with coupons and discounts, avoiding large, pricey purchases, paying all of your bills on time, and so on would be beneficial.

By completing all of this, you would become an educated individual who strives for a joyful and bright future rather than a miser. Therefore, saving money is a strategy for future security rather than turning you into a miser.

How to Cut Costs Without Being Stingy

It can be difficult to save money, particularly if you've set a standard of living. It is possible to be economical without giving up on the things you love, even though doing so can be quite unpleasant. The following advice will help you be economical without coming across as stingy:

Even for something as seemingly costly as designer pants or a new high-end blender, set aside money and save for it. If you are certain that you can afford your purchase, you will enjoy it much more.

For more expensive products, compare prices: frugal shoppers do their homework before making a purchase. The best deal might not always be found at your favorite store. Aim for seasonal discounts and exercise patience. Make sure you're getting the most for your money.

Recognize when to spend money. You won't have fun on a family vacation if you save up all year for it only to eat peanut butter and worry about money the entire time. If you need a new coat, budget for one that fits properly and will endure for several years. Sometimes spending more will result in greater value.

Before making a purchase, ask yourself three questions: Do I need it? Shall I make use of it? Can I afford it because I want it so much? You can feel secure in your purchase if you can say "yes" to each of the three questions.

Make a compromise: If the kids insist on getting ice cream from the store but you'd rather save money, go food shopping. Producing your sundaes might be more enjoyable and less expensive. Being creative frees you from having to say no all the time.

Keep in mind the importance of family time and memories: When thrifty people are used to living on a tight budget, it can be difficult for them to pay for dinners out and hotel stays. Enjoy the time spent reestablishing contact and spending time together if you must travel for a family reunion; don't stress about the financial aspect of things. Time spent together cannot be quantified.

Take a moment to reflect: If you're not sure whether to buy something, put it back on the shelf. In a few days, you can always come back and grab it. Ask the store to keep it for you if it's the final item of that kind or size. Reducing impulsive behavior can help you prevent impulsive purchases.

Keeping track of your receipts will help you keep tabs on your spending and return items that are unnecessary or that don't fit you, such as misfitting clothing. To conveniently return items that I'm not sure I need or want, I occasionally set them aside.

Have a little snack before heading out to eat: Treating yourself to a special dinner once in a while is enjoyable. If you find it difficult to spend money on meals, have a little snack before you arrive, and then make an informed choice about your entrée. There are plenty of dishes that are big enough to share between the two. I occasionally order a salad and an appetizer since it offers me variety without breaking the bank.

Tell your kids the truth: Parents who merely want to save money can come across as stingy. "That's not in the budget this month," is how I like to tell my kids when they ask for something extra as I like to be honest. When we go out to dine as a family, we could declare up front that "everyone's drinking water," to avoid turning down the restaurant's specialty cocktails.

You may save money without compromising your way of life or enjoyment by using these strategies, particularly if you have a family.

Always keep an eye on your expenditures and seek out chances to save money wherever you can.

This chapter has covered several topics, including how to increase your cash flow through wise savings and investments, how to expand your money without becoming a miser, and several approaches to financial development.

I'll go over how to safeguard your financial future with insurance, estate planning, and retirement planning in the upcoming chapter.

So, let's go out on this adventure in the following section of the book.

PART III

Playing the Long Game

Chapter 5
Future-Proofing Your Wallet

It's not how much money you make, but how much money you keep, how hard it works for you, and how many generations you keep it for. --Robert Kiyosaki

Let's be honest: none of us can predict what lies ahead in the future. However, having a solid financial foundation not only brings peace of mind but also makes it easier to navigate the unexpected twists and turns that life may throw our way. Even if you currently have your finances in a good place, it's always wise to be proactive and safeguard the hard-earned money you've accumulated. We've all witnessed the impact of market downturns, recessions, and global crises, which have taught us that no one is immune to economic upheaval. While having an emergency fund and savings can offer some level of security against financial pressures, they may not be sufficient if the problems persist for an extended time.

When financial misfortune strikes, it affects everyone, regardless of their social class or economic standing. Unless we are well-prepared, we are left vulnerable to uncertainty. Even those who have taken precautions can find their immunity tested. Financial misfortune can manifest in various ways, such as a global pandemic, sudden job loss, the closure of a business, a family breakdown like divorce, or even a significant health condition that requires long-term treatment.

Just like carrying an umbrella with you on a winter's day, in case it rains, in this chapter, I will guide you on how to future-proof your money and set yourself up for financial success.

Retirement Planning: The Earlier, The Better

When you're in your 30s and 40s, retirement may still seem like a distant event. You have other priorities, such as saving for a house, buying a car, paying off student debt, and saving for your child's college education. However, there are several benefits to starting a retirement fund early. Luckily, many employers and organizations offer retirement savings plans, so you can begin saving as soon as you start earning a salary. Here, I will provide you with some reasons why planning for retirement early is important.

Higher Returns on Your investments

By starting to save for retirement early, you have more time for your investments to grow and take advantage of compound interest. Compound interest is the interest you earn on your initial sum plus any previously accumulated interest or earnings. Over time, this can accumulate two thousands of dollars. To get an idea of how powerful compound interest can be when starting retirement planning early, you can use a compound interest calculator.

A thirty-year-old professional making a $80,000 salary can collect about $1.5 million by the time she reaches sixty-five years old if she begins contributing ten per cent of her income through her 401(k) at thirty. (Presuming a yearly average of 6% investment returns and a 3% pay increase).

You Can Make Riskier Investment Decisions

Generally speaking, the investments with the highest potential rates of return also entail the largest level of risk. Generally speaking, the younger you are, the more risk you can accept with your investments in a 401(k) or other retirement account. This is because you will have enough time to recuperate from your losses. It is often wiser to switch to a more cautious approach as you approach retirement.

Riskier decisions have greater potential rewards, but they also carry a greater danger of significant value swings. When you are building your investing portfolio, it is crucial to consider your risk tolerance.

Get a Sooner Retirement

Although 65 is the typical retirement age, you could wish to start your retirement earlier. Once you have paid off all of your debts and saved enough money, you can choose to retire early. You may be able to achieve your retirement objective sooner in life if you comprehend the significance of retirement planning and carry out an investment strategy.

Many retirees go on to pursue hobbies or new jobs that they weren't able to fit in while working a 9–5 job. Committing to saving for retirement in your early years might lead to greater freedom and flexibility in your later years.

Retirement May Result in Lower Housing Expenses

You won't have to worry about living close to your place of employment or about the expense of your commute after you retire. The decision of where to live will be more up to you. Real estate in smaller rural villages is frequently less expensive than in larger metropolis. This might allow you to pay off any outstanding mortgage and relocate to a less expensive home.

Benefit From Employer Contributions

Make sure you invest enough to take full benefit of any employer match offered on your 401(k) contributions if your employer offers to match. For instance, if you contribute 5% of your salary or more to your 401(k), your company might match 50% of your contributions. This implies that your employer would pay an additional $1,750 to your 401(k) if you make $70,000 annually and contribute $3,500. During your working life, this can add up to a significant amount of money—basically, free money. Your retirement savings will be substantially increased if you begin making contributions to a 401(k) with an employer match early in your career.

Social Security Benefits Are Not Assured

The average monthly Social Security income is about $1,500. That could not be sufficient to maintain your standard of living in retirement and pay your bills. The program's reserves may run out of money entirely by 2034, at which point payouts could be reduced by 22%. You should have your retirement funds so you aren't dependent on social security, even though this could alter.

When Should I Begin Making Retirement Plans?

In a nutshell, as soon as you can. This is so that your money has more time to grow the earlier you start saving. The argument that they are too young to start saving for retirement is one of the most used ones. Anyone who is getting close to retirement will attest that time flies fast and that the longer you put off investing, the tougher it is to accumulate a retirement nest egg.

Less than $5,000 is saved by over 40% of Americans for retirement. As they get closer to retirement, this will cause them a great deal of financial worry. An earlier start can lessen this strain and result in a more contented retirement.

What Are the Initial Stages of Planning for Retirement?

Decide on the retirement income you wish to have. This will primarily rely on the kind of lifestyle you wish to lead. You won't require as much if your retirement plan is to live a tranquil country lifestyle as opposed to an international traveler.

Put your financial objectives first. Your savings objectives certainly extend beyond retirement. A fiduciary financial advisor can be useful in this situation. It's critical to assess your financial objectives holistically and devise a plan of action to meet each one.

Choose the retirement savings plan that best suit your needs. The greatest retirement plans typically offer extra savings incentives, including matching contributions, along with tax benefits.

This is how retirement planning is generally approached. Consulting with a professional financial planner could be a fantastic way for you to do a more thorough examination of your retirement.

Retirement Schemes

There are numerous sizes and shapes for retirement accounts. There might be differences in the guidelines and policies for each. I'll go over some of the different retirement plans with you, along with how to sign up for them.

Plans Sponsored by Employers

Plans such as the 403(b) or 401(k) offered by employers are excellent options for young individuals. Major firms offer a type of retirement account known as the former. The latter is a comparable approach that some nonprofit organizations and staff members of public schools follow. Both operate in comparable ways.

One advantage of these qualifying retirement plans right now is that, up to a certain level, your employer may match your contributions. For instance, your employer might match your 3% yearly income contribution to your plan account and deposit the same amount into your retirement account, thereby giving you a 3% annual bonus that increases over time.

It is recommended that you make a larger contribution than what the company will match. Experts suggest going above 10%. Under 50-year-olds can fund a 401(k) or 403(b) with up to $22,500 of their earnings this year and $23,000 the following year; an employer may match some of these contributions. An additional $7,500 can be contributed annually by those over 50 as a catch-up payment this year and in subsequent years.

A better rate of return than a savings account is one of the 401(k) plans' additional benefits (although the investments are not risk-free).

Income tax does not apply to the money in the account until you take it out. You will immediately receive a tax benefit on your income because your donations are deducted from your gross income. People who are about to enter a higher tax rate can think about making a large enough contribution to reduce their tax obligation.

Conventional IRAs/Individual Retirement Accounts

You can use a standard individual retirement account (IRA) to save pre-tax money. This implies that your savings are subtracted from your income before the application of taxes. It therefore reduces your taxable income and, consequently, your tax obligation. Therefore, investing in a traditional IRA can lower your tax bracket if you're about to enter one.

This type of account has an upfront tax benefit. You are therefore liable to pay your regular tax rate at the time you collect distributions from the account. But remember that the funds increase in an interest-bearing manner. Until you start taking withdrawals, the amount of your account is not subject to dividend or capital gains taxes.

The annual contribution amount to a traditional IRA is capped by the IRS. Inflation is used to determine this amount. An extra $1,000 can be invested by those 50 years of age and above, for a total of $7,500.

Distributions can be made as early as 59½ and must be taken at age 72. If you take out money before then, there's a 10% penalty. Additionally, taxes will be due at your standard income tax rate.

Account for Individual Retirement (IRA) in Roth

With post-tax funds, a Roth IRA can be a great tool for young adults. This avoids the larger income tax hit when the money is withdrawn in retirement but does away with the immediate tax deduction. Even if you don't have much money to contribute initially, opening a Roth IRA early can pay off greatly in the long term. Recall that greater tax-free interest is earned the longer money is left in a retirement account.

Roth IRAs are not without restrictions. The annual contribution cap for an IRA (regular or Roth) is $6,500, or $7,500 if you are over 50.

A Roth IRA carries penalties for withdrawing funds before reaching retirement age, just like a 401(k). However, there are a few noteworthy exclusions that could be extremely helpful for younger individuals or in an emergency. First of all, there is never a penalty if you decide to withdraw the initial amount you invested. Second, you can take out money for specific educational fees, a down payment on a first house, medical expenses, and disability payments.

Account for Individual Retirement (IRA) - SIMPLE

Employees of small enterprises can opt for the SIMPLE IRA as a retirement account instead of the more costly 401(k) plan. Employers can choose to match employee contributions, and employees can save money automatically through payroll deductions like a 401(k).

This sum is limited to three per cent of the worker's yearly pay. For a SIMPLE IRA, the maximum yearly contribution is $15,500 in the first year and $16,000 in the second.

Retirement Planning Stages

Here are some pointers for effective retirement planning at various life phases.

Young Adulthood (25-35 Years Old)

Even though they might not have a lot of extra cash to spend, newlyweds have time to allow their assets to grow, which is an important and worthwhile component of retirement savings. The compounding principle is to blame for this.

Interest can earn interest thanks to compound interest, and the longer you have, the more interest you will accrue. The magic of compounding means that even if you can only save $50 a month if you invest it at age 25 it will be worth three times as much as if you wait until age 45. You may always invest more money down the road, but you can never make up for missed time.

Early Midlife
(36–50 Years Old)

Financial burdens associated with early midlife typically include credit card debt, mortgages, college loans, and insurance payments. At this point in the retirement planning process, it is imperative to keep saving. These are some of the strongest years for aggressive savings because of the combination of earning more money and the amount of time you still have to invest and earn interest. At this point in their retirement planning, people should keep taking advantage of any employer-sponsored 401(k) matching programme. Additionally, they ought to make an effort to fund their Roth IRA or 401(k) to the maximum (you can have both at the same moment). If you're not qualified for a Roth IRA, you might want to think about a standard IRA. This is funded with pretax cash, just like your 401(k), and the assets grow tax-deferred.

A Roth option is available for setting aside after-tax retirement contributions in certain employer-sponsored plans. There are no income restrictions unlike with a Roth IRA, but you are still subject to the same annual maximum.

Lastly, don't overlook disability and life insurance. If something were to happen to you, you want to be sure your family could get by without having to take money out of your retirement accounts.

Later Midlife (50–65 Years Old)

Your investment accounts ought to get increasingly cautious as you get older. T-bills, or Treasury notes, are among the safest investments, but they also have one of the lowest yields when considering alternative options.

There are a few benefits, but for those in this stage of retirement planning, time is running out to save. Increased income and possibly the repayment of some of the previously mentioned debt (credit card debt, school loans, mortgages, etc.) by this point can free up more cash for investing.

Additionally, opening and funding an IRA or 401(k) is something you can do at any time. Catch-up contributions are one advantage of this stage of retirement planning. You can add $1,000 more to your regular or Roth IRA and $7,500 more to your 401(k) per year once you turn 50. If you have used all of your tax-advantaged retirement savings choices, you might want to think about adding to your retirement savings with other types of investments. Investing in blue-chip stocks, CDs, or certain real estate properties (such as a vacation house you rent out) could be a pretty safe method to increase your nest egg.

Additionally, you can start to estimate how much your Social Security benefits will be and when it will make sense for you to begin receiving them. The full retirement age for benefits is 66, however, eligibility for early benefits begins at age 62. Now is also the ideal moment to research long-term care insurance, which can assist with paying for in-home care or a nursing home if you require it as you age. Health-related costs, particularly those that come as a surprise, can completely deplete your funds if you do not adequately plan for them.

There is much more to retirement planning than just calculating how much you will need and save. It considers your entire financial situation.

Your Home

The majority of Americans consider their home to be their most valuable possession. What role does that play in your retirement strategy? In the past, planners saw a home as an asset; but, following the housing market meltdown, that view has changed. Rather than retiring with a large amount of money, many homeowners are entering retirement with mortgage debt due to the growing popularity of home equity loans and home equity lines of credit (HELOCs). The issue of whether to sell your house after you retire also needs to be considered. It may be more than you need if you continue to live in the house where you raised several children, and maintaining it may come with high costs. An objective assessment of your house and your retirement plan should be part of it.

Estate Planning

Your estate plan specifies what will happen to your assets after your death. It should include a will outlining your intentions, but even before that, you should establish a trust or adopt another technique to protect as much of it as possible from inheritance taxes.

As of 2024, the first $13.61 million of inheritance is exempt from estate taxes, but more and more people are discovering ways to leave money to their children in a way that does not pay them in one flat payment. There may also be changes in the works in Congress addressing inheritance taxes since the estate tax threshold is set to be reduced to $5 million by 2026.

Tax Efficiency

When you reach retirement age and begin receiving distributions, taxes become a significant issue. Most of your retirement accounts are subject to regular income tax. This means you might pay up to 37% in taxes on any money you withdraw from your regular 401(k) or IRA.

That is why it is critical to consider a Roth IRA or a Roth 401(k), as both allow you to pay taxes beforehand rather than at withdrawal. If you anticipate you will make more money later in life, you may want to consider a Roth conversion. An accountant or financial planner can assist you with such tax considerations.

Insurance

Asset protection is a critical component of retirement planning. Age brings more medical costs, and you'll have to navigate the often-complicated Medicare system. Many people believe that traditional Medicare does not provide adequate coverage, so they seek a Medicare Advantage or Medigap policy to augment it. There are also life and long-term care insurance options to consider.

An annuity is another form of policy that an insurance company may provide. An annuity is similar to a pension. You put money on deposit with an insurance provider, which then pays you a specified monthly amount. Annuities come in a variety of alternatives, and there are numerous factors to consider when considering if they are ideal for you.

How Do I Begin Planning for Retirement?

Retirement planning is not tough. It's as simple as saving a little money each month—every little bit helps. The simplest approach is to begin contributing through an employer-sponsored plan if your firm provides one. You may also wish to consult with an expert, such as a financial planner or investment broker, who can guide you in the proper route. The earlier you begin, the better. That's because your investments expand over time as they generate interest. And you will earn interest on your interest.

Why Is Retirement Planning So Important?

Retirement planning allows you to save enough money to continue your current lifestyle. After all, no one wants to keep working until the very end. While you may work part-time or take up odd jobs, it is unlikely that you will be able to sustain your existing lifestyle. Social Security funds will only get you so far. That is why it is critical to have a feasible plan in place that will allow you to retire with the most money possible.

What Other Factors Should I Consider During Retirement?

Retirement planning is an essential aspect of your financial well-being. However, there are other factors to consider aside from what happens once you retire. Ensure that your finances provide you with the most tax breaks available, so a Roth conversion may be a good choice if you feel you will be earning money later in life. You may also want to think about what happens to your assets after your death, which is where estate planning comes in. If you are wounded or die unexpectedly, life insurance can assist cover any expenses left for your loved ones.

So, what I'm saying is that everyone dreams of the day when they can finally say goodbye to their jobs and retire. However, doing so costs money. This is the point at when retirement planning is important. It doesn't matter where you are in life. Sure, you may receive Social Security benefits, but they may not be sufficient, especially if you are accustomed to a certain lifestyle. Setting away money today will leave you with less to worry about later.

Estate Planning and Wills Are Not Just for the Elderly and Wealthy

Many people believe that estate planning is only for the "elderly" and the "wealthy." However, estate planning does much more than only distribute assets, prevent probate, and plan for taxes. An estate plan is a set of instructions given to persons you trust to make decisions for you during times of disability and to transfer your assets after your death. Estate planning manifests itself in the most fundamental forms: distribution-guiding papers (wills and trusts), healthcare directives, and financial powers of attorney.

What constitutes a will? A will name a personal representative and instruct her to transfer your assets after your death. A will can also name a guardian and conservator for your minor and/or adult children if one is required.

What is a revocable living trust? A revocable living trust is a separate legal body that "holds" property and is administered by a trustee (you) for your benefit while you are alive. Your successor trustee, or anyone you name, divides your estate in accordance with your wishes after your passing. You can customize your trust to match your specific distribution needs, which can frequently be as complex as you like. A trust can provide for you (and your loved ones) if you become disabled. It can also tell your successor trustee to give financial support to your minor children until they reach adulthood.

What is a healthcare directive? Healthcare directives (sometimes known as "living wills") designate someone to make end-of-life healthcare decisions for you when you are unable to do so, and they also influence that person's actions to meet your wishes. These cover religious wishes, family or other matters, life support and treatment requests, and more.

What are the financial powers of attorney? Financial powers of attorney enable you to appoint someone to act on your behalf about your property and finances. Powers of attorney can be immediate (giving authority to your agent instantly) or springing (taking effect only after you become incapacitated).

Whether you are 20 or 90 years old, you have loved ones (children, spouse, dependent parents, friends, etc.) and assets to care for and manage. But who will care for you and your possessions if you become handicapped or die? Without a written estate plan, you leave your loved ones with numerous tough and personal decisions. By drafting an estate plan, you prepare for your loved ones when you die, someone is already designated to enforce your healthcare and financial intentions when you are unable to do so, and explicit instructions require a personal representative or trustee to transfer your hard-earned assets as you specify.

Death is unpleasant to plan for, but failing to plan may put your family in a difficult situation. Creating an estate plan will protect your wishes, family, and assets. The process of creating arrangements for the administration and transfer of your estate following your passing, utilizing a will, trust, insurance policies, and/or other tools, is the most widely understood definition of estate planning. Although estate planning has been practiced for a while, its acceptance is growing.

There are many aspects to estate planning, but the first step is to undertake a thorough analysis of your estate assets. Your estate consists of all the property you possess, including:

- Cash
- Cars
- Clothing
- Jewelry
- Houses
- Investments.
- Savings.
- Retirement accounts.
- Land
- And more.

After you've determined the components of your estate, you may begin planning.

Basics of Estate Planning

Estate planning is crucial for a variety of reasons. The biggest advantage is probably this: if you don't make enough plans while you're still well and able to anticipate future events, you won't be able to control how your estate is managed or what your loved ones inherit when the time comes. Planning today assures that your tomorrow is exactly as you imagine it.

A well-designed Estate Plan will precisely spell down your preferences in the most tax-efficient manner, ensuring that there will be no questions, misunderstandings, or misconceptions about what you want.

Most Common Estate Planning Documents

Your estate plan will consist of several documents. Each has its significance, and when combined, they provide a powerful picture of your dying wishes.

Guardianship

State your wishes and who you want to care for your children or any other dependents you are accountable for after your death or if you are no longer able to care for them. Instructions for guardianship are typically contained in a part of your will.

Will

A legal document in which you express your final desires for the distribution of your property or other assets.

Trust

A legally binding fiduciary agreement between three parties whereby the first, known as the Settlor, also grants the second, known as the Trustee, the power to hold assets and property for the benefit of the third, known as the Beneficiary.

Financial Power of Attorney (POA)

A legal document granting someone the authority to handle your financial affairs.

Durable Power of Attorney (POA)

A version of a Financial Power of Attorney, which is a document that grants another person legal authority to handle any of your non-health or non-medical matters. "Durable" merely implies that even if you become incapacitated, the POA will remain in effect.

Advanced Healthcare Directive (AHCD)

Also known as a Living Will or Medical Power of Attorney. An Advance Healthcare Directive specifies what medical actions should be taken if you become incapacitated and unable to make your own decisions.

It is vital to realize that, while the terms "Living Will," "Medical Power of Attorney," and "AHCD" are sometimes used interchangeably, there are legal distinctions between them.

- A Living Will allows you to indicate your medical preferences, particularly for end-of-life decisions such as life support.
- A Medical Power of Attorney designates someone to make healthcare choices for you if you are unable to do so.
- An AHCD combines the Living Will and Medical Power of Attorney, allowing you to express instructions while also designating someone else to make choices for you if necessary.

HIPAA Authorization

Consent you grant to share your medical data or information with a third party.

Estate Planning and Taxes

Taxes play a significant role in estate planning. Giving your heirs as much as possible is the ultimate goal. Strategizing and taking action to reduce assets lost to taxes is an effective strategy to reach your goal. There are various instruments you can utilize in your Estate Plan, such as ways to avoid probate and transfer assets while avoiding high taxes. Understanding the many sorts of taxes is crucial.

- **Estate tax:** A tax imposed on estates above a certain value. The tax is only levied on the amount that exceeds the maximum, not the total worth of the estate.
- **Inheritance tax**: This is a tax paid by those who inherit property or money from a deceased individual.
- **Gift tax:** A tax imposed on gifts above a specified amount. It is important to note that any taxes are the responsibility of the giver, not the receiver.

Who Needs an Estate Plan?

Short answer: everyone. It's easy to tell ourselves that we don't need an estate plan. But, in reality, we would all benefit from more forward preparation. You don't have to be affluent, elderly, or have a specified amount in your bank account to explain the necessity for an

Estate Plan. If you are over the age of 18, you should begin thinking about developing a strategy.

Even if you don't have many assets, your Estate Plan ensures that everyone understands your preferences. Health directives and long-term healthcare requests are great instances of this; if you become incapacitated and unable to communicate your wishes, your Estate Plan will speak for you, saving your loved ones from having to make difficult decisions or wonder what you would want.

Previously, correctly drafting the types of paperwork that go into an Estate Plan may cost thousands of dollars. But you now have options. You can obtain an economical, legal, effective, and valid Estate Plan that ensures your preferences are known should the need arise. Even if you don't have many assets, an Estate Plan is still a good idea.

The 12-Step Guide to Drafting an Estate Plan

Yes, there are many processes involved in drafting a thorough Estate Plan, but I've made it as simple as possible for you by putting them all out.

1. **Collect your assets:** Inventory everything you own, including cars and collectibles.

2. **Protect your family:** Think about whether you have adequate life insurance to support your family's way of life going forward

3. **Determine which plan is best for you:** Choose the sort of Estate Plan you require.

4. **Choose who you want to be the guardian of your children, pets, or yourself:** If you have children or pets, or if you care for a loved one who is unable to care for themselves, you should select a guardian. You can also specify who you would like to make medical and/or financial decisions on your behalf if you become unable to do so for yourself.

5. **Determine and implement the appropriate directives:** You should include the following directives in your Estate Plan:
   - Durable Power of Attorney.
   - Medical care directive.
   - Limited Power of Attorney (LPOA) is less typically utilized than Durable Power of Attorney (DPO), but can still be useful in certain situations.

6. **Name your beneficiaries:** Some documents and accounts will already have Beneficiaries listed. Retirement plans and life insurance policies, for example, could fall under this category. However, if you want to leave certain assets to a specific

individual, you should include them in your will or trust. If there is an opportunity, you should specify contingent beneficiaries. Keep in mind that Beneficiary designations will only take effect after your death, so if you become disabled and unable to make decisions, you must have planned for more than just naming Beneficiaries.

7. **Find a trustworthy partner:** Examine your alternatives for developing an estate plan. This can be done in person with an attorney, or you can hire another service provider. You have options, but some will be significantly more expensive than others.

8. **Create a plan:** If you're using an online program to build your Estate Plan, make sure you complete all of the processes and finalize everything.

9. **Sign and notarize your estate plan:** Remember to check your state's requirements for the number of witnesses.

10. Notify your executor: It is a good idea to inform the person you have chosen as your Executor of your plans.

11. **Keep track of your estate planning documents:** Put your Estate Plan in a secure location where your loved ones may quickly access it. A fireproof safe is an excellent idea.

12. **Update as needed over time:** There is no hard rule for when you should update your Estate Plan, but a decent rule of thumb is to update it whenever a significant life event occurs. And, if you haven't experienced any significant life events in the last few years, attempt to evaluate and revise your plan every three to five years.

Common Estate Planning Mistakes to Avoid

When creating an estate plan, proceed with prudence. Numerous mistakes could cause delays, inaccuracies, or other misconceptions. Some of the most common mistakes people make along the journey are:

- No official strategy in place.
- Failure to update plans for significant life events.
- Failure to plan for future incapacities, such as disability or long-term care.
- Improper asset ownership (easiness of passing assets on)
- Excludes charitable gifts.
- Failure to appoint a guardian for vulnerable individuals, such as children.
- Underestimating the impact of taxes.
- Lack of asset liquidity.

- Preventing lifetime gifts from lowering estate value for tax purposes.
- Adding a child's name to property deeds may have significant tax effects.

The Difference Between an Estate Plan and a Will

While many individuals believe that simply possessing a will is enough, the truth is that you need more. If you have a Will, you are off to a good start. However, a Will is only a minor element of the estate planning puzzle. To properly safeguard your loved ones after your death, you must include any paperwork, nominations, and appointments to guarantee you have done everything possible to make the process easy for them when the time comes.

Frequently Asked Questions on Estate Planning

- **What are Beneficiary Designations?**

A beneficiary designation is a technique to specify where your assets should go after your death.

- **What does a Trustee do?**

A Trustee manages all of the assets or property of a Trust. In essence, he or she is the legal owner of those goods.

- **How Much Does Estate Planning Cost?**

The cost of drafting an estate plan might vary greatly based on a variety of things. If you choose the traditional approach and deal with an attorney in person, your costs will be significantly higher.

- **When making an estate plan, do I need an Attorney?**

In some situations, you may not need an attorney to draft your estate plan. If you have a complicated estate, you may choose the traditional face-to-face approach. Though there are many aspects to a complete Estate Plan, handling them one at a time is the best approach to designing a plan that is conclusive, comprehensive, and thorough, as well as protecting everyone in your life you care about.

So far, you've seen that estate planning is a vital aspect of your financial strategy, and it can help you secure your most valuable possessions. With a comprehensive estate plan, you can ensure that your desires are carried out after your death, provide for people who rely on you financially, protect your family from hefty probate fees, and more.

Insurance: Protecting Your Financial Future

As we move through life, we frequently take for granted the things we have and the people we love. However, have you ever considered what may happen if something unexpected occurred? You could think you don't need insurance, but believe me, you do. In this section, we will look at why insurance is important for protecting your financial future and how to ensure you are insured.

Why Insurance Matters

Before we go into the details of insurance, let's talk about why it's important. When you think about insurance, you may see automobile accidents or healthcare, but it is much more than that. Insurance protects you against the unexpected, such as a natural disaster, a lawsuit, or just losing your job.

It provides a safety net, ensuring that you do not bear the entire financial burden of a disaster. Without insurance, you risk depleting your funds, going into debt, or losing your home or other possessions.

Types of Insurance to Consider

So, what kinds of insurance should you consider? Let me share you some of the most popular types:

1. **Health insurance** - There is no debate. You need health insurance because you never know when you'll need it. From routine check-ups to emergency procedures, health insurance

can help you cover medical expenditures that would otherwise be unaffordable.

2. **Life insurance-** This is often obtained to provide for your loved ones in the case of your untimely demise. It can aid with funeral expenditures, debt repayment, or simply provide a financial cushion to assist your loved ones in getting back on their feet.

3. **Homeowners or Renters Insurance** - Whether you own a home or rent a flat, having insurance to protect your property is crucial. Homeowners insurance protects your home and its belongings against theft, fire, and natural catastrophes. Renters insurance protects your personal belongings in the case of a comparable incident.

4. **Auto Insurance** - If you own a car, you need to have auto insurance. Most states require it by law, and it protects you in the event of a car accident, theft, or other misfortune.

5. **Disability Insurance** - If you become disabled and unable to work, disability insurance will provide you with a stable income. It can help you pay your payments and keep your current lifestyle at a difficult moment.

Ensuring Your Coverage

Now that you've determined which types of insurance to consider, how can you ensure you're covered? Here are some tips:

1. **Do Your Research:** Not all insurance policies are made equal. Make sure to conduct your research and compare policies from several firms to get one that meets your demands and budget.
2. **Don't Skimp on Coverage:** While it may be tempting to choose the cheapest coverage available, doing so may result in higher long-term costs. Make sure you have adequate coverage to safeguard yourself in the event of an unexpected crisis.
3. **Review Your Policies Annually:** As your life changes, so will your insurance needs. Make sure to examine your policies on an annual basis to verify that they continue to fulfil your needs.
4. **Consider Working with a Trusted Advisor:** If you're not sure what types of insurance you need or how much coverage you should have, consider hiring a trusted advisor to help you navigate the process.

Insurance is vital for securing your financial future. There are several different types of insurance to consider, including health insurance, life insurance, home insurance, and auto insurance. Do your research, don't skimp on coverage, evaluate your plans periodically, and consult with a trustworthy advisor to ensure you have the protection you require. By taking these proactive steps, you may help protect your financial future and get a piece of mind along the way.

This chapter has covered a variety of ways to protect your financial future, including retirement planning, estate planning and wills, and insurance.

You may wonder, "What if I run into difficulties when implementing the numerous methods of protecting my financial future?". In the following chapter, we will look in depth at how to overcome financial hurdles that may come your way.

Let's go!...

Chapter 6

When Life Throws You a Curveball

*I have not failed. I've just found 10,000 ways that won't work. --
Thomas A. Edison*

It may happen to any of us—we suddenly find ourselves overtaken by sadness. Perhaps we suffered a catastrophic loss. Perhaps we've reached a breaking point. Or perhaps we are facing a sudden and unexpected upheaval.

Coping with life's unexpected twists and turns comprises three parts:

1) Stop and recover.

2) Plan.

3) Follow through on new habits and routines.

Sometimes, things happen in life that significantly impact us, especially when we are not expecting them. Things like this can cause our moods to swing dramatically. We can experience fear and anxiety.

It can be difficult to think. Difficult to concentrate. The fight-or-flight reflex kicks in.

Occasionally, life throws you a curveball that directly or indirectly impacts your finances: you're laid off, your furnace fails, or you're having a child and realize you'll need to renovate your dwellings soon.

The last thing you want to do is dig deeper because you couldn't handle your finances properly.

In this chapter, I will lead you through numerous tactics for overcoming financial setbacks, learning from past financial mistakes you or others have made, and being resilient during economic downturns.

So, let us proceed!...

Overcoming Financial Setbacks

We all want to avoid them, but financial setbacks are a sad reality of life. Almost everyone has faced a financial setback at some point in their lives. We lose our jobs, and a medical emergency leaves us with massive bills, or another catastrophic calamity compels us to deplete our funds. Whatever the cause of the financial setback, you must be honest about your circumstances to move forward and regain control. The sooner you address the issues, the sooner you can begin your recovery.

You may think your circumstance is exceptional, but it is pretty common. It's so prevalent that there are several crucial, tried-and-true strategies to help you recover if you suffer a financial setback. Here, I'll walk you through the actions you can take to overcome any financial setbacks you're experiencing or may encounter.

Know You Are Not Alone

Things like this will happen to everyone at least once in their lives; your friends, neighbors, and relatives have all experienced them. There is no shame in having unpredictable; unforeseen situations affect you or make a few poor decisions that result in a terrible outcome. However, you can choose how you respond, making a huge difference in your financial recovery.

Understand Your Options

Find a balance between being upset and considering your financial condition. A clear, detailed look at what you have accessible will assist you in planning or determining what you can pursue. It may also encourage creativity, resilience, and a sense of accomplishment.

Reset Your Budget

Whatever the financial setback, you must figure out how to budget moving ahead. For example, if you had to accept a pay reduction or switch to a lower-paying job, you must recalculate how you wish to spend your remaining income. If you incurred a huge expense and now have monthly debt obligations, you must plan how to lower your spending in other areas to compensate for the cost. "Return to basics, modify your costs to match your income level after the setback, and build the surplus to get back on track.

Focus on the Future

Remember that your financial setback does not have to define the rest of your life; knowing this might help you stay motivated as you fight to repair your finances. Understand that a setback is merely a temporary setback. Many successful people experienced failures but persevered. Henry Ford declared bankruptcy twice before revolutionizing manufacturing. As part of your recovery strategy, try setting milestones where you reward yourself in some way, such as going out for a nice dinner — or doing anything else you enjoy — if you reach particular amounts in your emergency fund. In this manner, you not only save money, but you also motivate yourself to do so.

Reduce
Excess Expenses

Don't wait until your bank account reaches zero to reduce spending wherever feasible. Once you know what's coming on, such as a wage cut, cutting your costs before it happens will help you stay afloat for longer. For example, you might cancel your cable and fitness center memberships until the early termination fee makes them prohibitively expensive. Similarly, if you have a landline and a mobile, you may use one to save money. Selling one automobile when you already have two can help you save money. Not only does this provide extra income, but it also saves you money on insurance and registration payments.

Planning
for the Future

Create a strategy to reduce the likelihood of another financial setback significantly impacting your finances in the future. No strategy is guaranteed to withstand every potential financial setback, but planning for the future can lessen the likelihood of future setbacks having such a devastating impact. I advocate setting up an emergency fund for six months' living expenses. For example, if your rent, food, transportation, and other expenses total $2,100 monthly, you should set aside $12,600 for financial emergencies. I also recommend getting insurance to cover "catastrophic losses" and avoiding consumer debt, such as holding balances on credit cards. Finally, put at least 20% down when purchasing a home.

Financial losses are about more than just the amount of money lost. They can shake your entire belief system. However, they are manageable and allow you to reassess what is most essential in your life.

Learn from Financial Mistakes

We often deal with regret. Personal finance involves various decisions concerning earning, saving, and investing. Assuming 30 years of labor and 20 years of retirement, we make financial decisions for 50 years or more. What are the chances we will always get it right? We are all prone to making mistakes, and they happen too frequently for comfort. It's either we learn from our mistakes or we don't. We repeat mistakes without understanding why. For example, some of us cannot resist investing in IPOs or betting on penny stocks. Sometimes, we make money and brag about it; sometimes, we lose money and want to forget it. However, we cannot resist when we encounter another "opportunity." Researchers who have studied our blunders highlight a crucial contrast. There does not appear to be an issue with how our brain processes information. When deciding, we tend to follow previous experience-based guidelines. In reality, we make better use of our brain's resources by automating certain rule-based processes, allowing us to complete them nearly automatically and without effort. We apply the brake when the traffic light goes red, for example, without thinking about it.

The difficulty, however, appears to lie in the noise connected with the information we feed the brain. Or the amount and quality of information we incorporate into our thought processes. When we selectively add new variables to an equation, we get it wrong and make an error. If we liked a penny stock because it had a low PE multiple, we would stick with it until we were hit with a stock with poor-quality earnings and a low PE. We become suspicious of low PEs, yet penny stocks continue to pique our curiosity as we selectively applaud how some became multi-baggers. We then look for another way to identify them. If personal financial decisions contained options, and those choices resulted in different outcomes, it would be difficult to separate good quality information from bad, resulting in a noisy process every time we made a decision. Then, our outcomes and experiences would differ, and we would have no lessons to employ in the future. That is why most personal financial advice is rule-based, even if it is too broad to apply equally to everyone. Consider some of the rules commonly advocated in personal finance: save before you spend; spend within your means and don't borrow; insure before you invest; invest your savings in a diversified portfolio; invest for the long term; do not withdraw your investments unless necessary; do not time the markets; allocate assets based on need; set specific goals; save for retirement; and so on. Each rule entails a trade-off and a decision that can end in either reward or regret. The topic of how much savings is adequate has yet to be adequately answered. Many households cannot determine whether they are saving enough or overdoing it and depriving themselves of the pleasures of spending. Most households borrow to buy a home; many upgrade their cars with loans; credit cards are commonly used, and the occasional indulgence that exceeds the ability to pay is dealt with discreetly. Loans allow you to spend tomorrow's money today, and it's difficult to determine which is a mistake: taking a loan or refusing to take one at all. As you study the regulations, you will see that there is ample evidence for and against their implementation. Such information is frequently found in interactions with colleagues and acquaintances, in the news and media, and in market-based financial advice. Personal finance decisions are made under information overload. As a result, the loop of making a decision, realizing it is incorrect, and then repeating it continues. What should you aim for?

First, avoid personal finance inertia. That is the option in which you choose to do nothing because you are afraid you will make a mistake. This bad choice is evidenced by many people's high savings bank account balances, which they bear with quiet guilt. It is preferable to make mistakes than do nothing at all.

Second, when you make a mistake, pause to figure out what you can learn from it. Do not deny or blame anyone or anything, but reflect on what you could have done and why you did not. If you neglected to sell a stock that began to lose money, acknowledge this shortcoming and establish a stop loss limit the next time.

Third, understand your limitations while dealing with a mistake. You may be unwilling to curb your spending; you may be too tied to your property to consider anything else, or you may associate day trading with enjoyable gambling, making it difficult to give up. Every error provides an opportunity to reflect on what should have been done and why you did not. You may be selective or biased while employing information.

Fourth, consider the potential that personal financial behaviors can be corrected at any time. Most of us earn, save, and spend progressively over time, except for a few lucky inheritors. We should be able to adjust for a poorly placed fixed deposit, an incorrectly chosen IPO, a bad insurance product, or an incorrect mutual fund. Do not put all of your life's earnings, savings, or investments at risk; it may be too costly to repair a mistake. Fifth, the benefit of regulations is that they simplify things. If it appeals to you, create a few guidelines and incorporate them into your financial routines. You may wind up with a cautious default position that provides a safety net for any other financial mistakes you may make. Don't let a mistake go to waste. Use it to see yourself from a new perspective and adjust your financial situation accordingly.

Learn From Evelyn's Financial Mistakes

How well do you know Evelyn Marie Adams, the American lottery winner who won the New Jersey Lottery twice, in 1985 and 1986, for more than $5.4 million (both prizes were paid out as mandatory annuities)? Hitting the lottery twice made her enormously wealthy and renowned. Nevertheless, she battled compulsive gambling, losing a lot of money in Atlantic City casinos and on several bets.

The impact was not as expected, despite Evelyn's fortune in winning the lottery twice. Evelyn found herself living in a caravan park two decades after her momentous victory, having run out of money.

Evelyn reflects on how she lost her money through gambling and poor financial decisions, saying, "Winning the lottery isn't always what it's cracked up to be. I achieved the American dream, but I also lost it. It was a really difficult fall. It's termed "rock bottom."

While sudden affluence can quickly provide financial stability and allow you to pursue your dreams unhindered, it can also present various challenges. Many people, including Evelyn, have struggled to cope with their unexpected wealth.

Unexpected Financial Gains Can Be Problematic

The initial stages of a sudden financial gain can be rather anxiety-inducing since it signifies a big life change that requires time for both your body and mind to adapt. Additionally, there is enormous pressure to make sensible financial choices with your newfound wealth.

Many people who receive a large sum of money unexpectedly are unlikely to keep any of it for more than a few years. Here are some recommendations for dealing with the stress of a financial windfall:

- **Allow yourself time to adapt:** Take the time you need to adjust to your new financial circumstances and figure out how you want to manage your money. Don't feel rushed to make decisions.

- **Seek guidance from a trusted individual:** Talking with a confidant, such as a friend, family member, or financial expert, can help you process your feelings and develop a financial strategy.
- **Avoid making rash financial decisions with your sudden income:** Take your time to contemplate and seek professional advice before making major purchases or investing. Don't be discouraged by mistakes; see them as opportunities to learn and keep moving forward. Patience is a skill that takes time to perfect.
- **Focus on your priorities:** Before you determine what you want to do with your money or how to protect your financial future, consider some fundamental behaviors that will help you manage your finances more effectively in the long run.

Managing and settling outstanding loans and liabilities is critical before making financial decisions or securing your financial future. One of the most effective financial strategies is using unexpected wealth to pay off high-interest debt.

Creating an emergency fund is another important way to use unexpected wealth. This fund, saved in a savings account, covers unexpected expenses such as job loss, medical bills, or car repairs. Having an emergency fund allows you to avoid accumulating debt or selling assets when faced with unexpected financial challenges.

Financial gurus recommend setting aside three to six months' living expenses in your emergency fund; however, if your employment has a higher risk of job loss or you have many dependents, you may want to save more.

After paying off high-interest debt and setting up an emergency fund, consider investing the remaining funds. Investing allows you to increase your wealth over time, which can help you achieve financial goals like saving for retirement or buying a home.

Numerous investment options are available, emphasizing the importance of selecting investments aligned with your risk tolerance and financial objectives. Risk tolerance refers to your ability to withstand losses, and individuals with a low-risk tolerance may choose more conservative investments like bonds. In contrast, those with a high-risk tolerance may be open to more volatile investments like stocks.

How Should You Manage Sudden Financial Gains?

In the current circumstances, making wise financial decisions and preparing oneself for unforeseen fortune is of heightened importance. The sudden acquisition of a considerable amount of money can be daunting, and mistakes made during this time may have long-term effects.

Create a thorough financial plan to help you make wise spending, saving, and investing decisions. Your plan should include clearly defined goals, a budget, and an investment strategy.

Identify your financial goals—are you striving for early retirement, homeownership, or entrepreneurship? Create a plan to achieve them.

Next, create a detailed budget to keep track of your spending and ensure that you stay within your means. Regularly update your budget to account for any adjustments to your financial circumstances.

Develop an investment strategy after determining how you want your money to work for you. Investing allows you to gradually increase your wealth over time, but choosing investments appropriate for your risk tolerance and financial goals is critical.

Seek expert advice. Consulting with a financial advisor is an excellent approach to ensure that you make prudent financial choices with your unanticipated wealth. A financial advisor can assist you in creating a customized financial plan that aligns with your specific needs and objectives and guides you to avoid common financial mistakes.

There are numerous resources available to help you learn about personal finance, including books, articles, websites, and online courses. Understanding personal finance is essential for making sound financial decisions and managing unexpected wealth.

Begin your financial education by learning the essentials, such as budgeting, saving, investing, and debt management. Several books, articles, and educational websites may help you understand these topics better.

Before investing in any funds, it's critical to understand the distinct characteristics, risks, and potential rewards associated with each type of investment. Various options include stocks, bonds, mutual funds, and real estate. Remember to stay current on financial news and articles, as they can help you stay informed about the newest financial trends and obtain insight into various financial goods and services.

Be cautious of your spending habits. Practicing caution with your expenditures is key when you come into a substantial sum of money.

While it may be tempting to overspend with newfound fortune, it's important to recognize that your financial plenty is not limitless.

Begin by creating a budget, which allows you to track your income and expenses and ensures that you live within your means. Instead of making impulsive purchases, it's best to wait a few days or weeks to see if the desired item is still a genuine priority. Adopt a 24-hour rule, allowing thoughtful consideration, evaluating necessity, and comparing prices from various retailers.

It is okay to deny requests for financial aid, even from friends and family, because you are not expected to meet everyone else's financial issues. It is also advantageous to decline such requests assertively.

Making prudent financial decisions with your unexpected wealth can ensure a secure and fulfilling financial future. However, such a sudden windfall should not encourage frivolous financial behavior; rather, it should warn against the unforeseen pitfalls that frequently accompany a sudden influx of money.

Resilience in Economic Downturns

Many people may react with intense emotions and uncertainty when unemployment rates rise, and the media keeps covering the dire state of the economy. However, most people adjust to challenging environments and circumstances that change their lives quickly.

What enables some people to "bounce back" while keeping others in a state of overwhelm? These high-stress times require resilience and the ability to adapt well to adversity. Resilience is a teachable skill that can help you get through the current crisis and any future family, relationships, or career issues. According to the American Psychological Association's Stress in America Survey, money is a significant source of stress for Americans. When you seem to be inundated by unfavorable news that affects your family's circumstances or that you think might do so in the future, it's normal to feel overwhelmed. You may, however, learn strategies to manage stress more effectively and strengthen your resilience. You may maintain and use your resilience by putting this challenging circumstance in a positive perspective. I'll give you some advice here on how to develop resilience during difficult times financially.

- **Recognizing Change as a Natural Part of Life:** The current economic climate may require you to modify your lifestyle or aspirations. You can concentrate on conditions you can change by accepting the ones that cannot be changed.

Having feelings and grieving for your losses is okay; it just requires that you pay attention to the emotions that arise on the inside as a result of loss. Losing your job and other possessions is difficult and emotionally taxing. At first, you can experience phases of dread, grief, and rage. An excellent place to start is just by becoming aware of the feelings in your body and letting them move through you. Tell others about some of this by sharing a glimpse of your experience.

- **Creating Links:** Maintaining positive relationships with friends, family, and others is crucial. Resilience is strengthened by accepting assistance and support from people who are interested in you and are willing to listen. Speak with people about your circumstances as often as you can. Make sure you apply for all the help for which you qualify. Participating in local groups such as civic or faith-based organizations can offer social support and aid in regaining hope for certain individuals.

- **Maintain Perspective:** You may experience days of feeling overburdened. Keep in mind that this emotion is fleeting and could potentially assist you in overcoming it. You can cultivate a positive mindset and lessen daily stress by focusing on what you want to achieve rather than what you fear.

- **Seek Out Opportunities and Helpers:** Going through a challenging circumstance, like an economic crisis, may teach people a lot about themselves. Take advantage of this difficult period to advance your career or personal development. Seek out organizations in your neighborhood or online that can support your passions and increase the chances that you can apply your best abilities.

- **Recognize the Positive Aspects of Your Life:** Resilient people count their blessings. You may write a thank-you note to the individuals in your life to express how much they mean to you. Alternatively, you could dedicate five or ten minutes each day to thinking back on one thing for which you are thankful. These straightforward methods can have a significant impact.

- **Sustain A Positive Attitude:** There is no going back from what has occurred. However, you may alter your interpretation and reaction to situations if you possess resilience. Switch off the news and visualize the kind of person you want to be and how you want to handle this. Create a symbol or vision that motivates you to proceed. During this period, establish an example for people to follow by being yourself.

- **Determine Your Strengths and Resources:** Pay attention to your strengths and resources and leverage them to solve problems. If you forget that, discover what qualities others find most admirable in you. We frequently ignore our assets and strengths to concentrate on our flaws. Now is the moment to turn that around and consider the resources we bring to the table and how we have previously addressed problems of a similar nature.

- **Speak With a Psychologist:** Managing stress alone can occasionally be terrifying and overpowering. It can be challenging to discuss or even bring up the subject of money with friends or relatives. You might wish to speak with a psychologist who has been educated to listen and offer support if you're still feeling overwhelmed.

Managing financial crises and unforeseen expenses, learning from financial blunders, and avoiding hazards have all been covered in this chapter. We also discussed how to weather a downturn in the economy. Because "Health is Wealth," understanding this and putting it into practice is a great way to maintain your financial situation and health.

In the final chapter, which is the next after this chapter. I'll show you how to stay knowledgeable and on top of your finances by developing new financial habits and staying educated.

So, let's journey together!

Chapter 7

Keeping Your Money Game Strong

A wise person should have money in their head, but not in their heart. --Jonathan Swift

Navigating the complex world of finance might seem like a challenging game to win. However, with the correct methods, anyone willing to learn and adapt may achieve financial freedom and win the money game. This final chapter will delve deeply into the most critical actionable methods for financial success. It will present you with a roadmap to better your economic well-being, safeguard your future, and genuinely learn how to win the game of money. Whether you're just starting your finances or want to improve your approach, these ideas can help you achieve financial autonomy and prosperity.

Staying Financially Educated and Informed

Being financially literate gives a person the tools and resources necessary to achieve financial security later in life. A lack of financial literacy can lead to various hazards, including accumulating unsustainable debt burdens due to poor spending decisions or failing to plan for the future. This, in turn, can result in poor credit, bankruptcy, home foreclosure, and other severe outcomes. To become financially literate, you must study and practice several skills, such as budgeting, debt management and repayment, and understanding credit and investment products. Basic measures you can take to enhance your finances include:

- Developing a budget.
- Keeping track of your expenses.
- Making timely payments.
- Conserving money wisely.
- Reviewing your credit report.
- Investing regularly for the future.
- Creating and Maintaining Good Financial Habits

Good financial habits are the foundation for creating money. Building financial freedom does not happen fast; it requires time and a foundation of solid habits that you practice daily.

No such thing as 'becoming rich quickly.' Yes, you can win the lottery, but most individuals lose their riches because they lack the skills to properly manage their newly acquired fortune.

When it comes to developing excellent financial habits, simplicity is vital. You want to give yourself the best chance of success by focusing on habits that you can achieve and, more importantly, sustain. This boosts your self-confidence and determination to pursue financial abundance.

I previously defined a habit as an acquired behavior repeated regularly until it becomes almost second nature. It's similar to learning to drive; it takes hours of practice to master. However, once you've acquired the technique, you'll find yourself coming home with no memory of the journey, owing to your autopilot usage.

Willpower and discipline are two essential characteristics for developing and maintaining new behaviors. When an action becomes habitual, a brain pathway is developed to reinforce the behavior. When you cultivate the activities that lead to wealth creation, they will quickly become second nature, causing you to naturally (habitually) do those things that can help you attain financial success.

We're all creatures of habit; just look at your daily routine: you probably clean your teeth, drink your morning coffee, and drive the same route to work daily. So, why is it so difficult to develop new healthy habits?

A person can acquire a new habit between 18 to 254 days, with an average of 66 days for a new behavior to become automatic. There is no one-size-fits-all method for developing new behaviors. In most cases, trial and error is required to determine what works best for you.

As previously stated, keeping things simple increases your chances of sticking to your new routines. Most people give up after a day or two because they believe continuing is pointless.

If you forget now and then, it has little effect on your capacity to create a new habit; what matters is that you continue and maintain discipline.

Start Small

Most people struggle to develop excellent habits because they set unsustainable lofty goals. If you have never been to the gym and expect to go five times a week without fail, you are in for a surprise.

For example, if you want to save for a house deposit, start by putting aside a tiny percentage of your salary, and after you're comfortable with that, re-evaluate your budget to see where you can cut back on spending to save more. The gratification you'll feel when you truly save what you say you'll save is unparalleled.

Try it Every Day

As real estate is a long-term investment, so is developing new habits. As previously stated, it takes approximately 66 days for an action to become habitual. Building healthy financial habits isn't as glamorous as most people believe; it takes modest measures each day that, over time, add up to a significant difference.

Make it Easy!

It's all about working smarter, not harder! Clearing the hurdles you may face increases your chances of forming a new habit. Humans are highly sensitive to little friction in our surroundings; thus, decreasing distractions will increase your chances of developing a new habit.

For example, if you want to learn more about wealth building through property investment, you may sign up for a real estate e-newsletter. Positive Real Estate offers a weekly email with the education you need to expand your property portfolio.

Reward Yourself

In our fast-paced environment, most individuals move on to the next thing without adequately acknowledging and celebrating their accomplishments. Rewards are a key aspect of habit-building.

Rewards educate us on what acts are worth remembering in the future. The brain is a reward detector. As you go about your daily routine, your nervous system constantly monitors which behaviors satisfy your desires and provide pleasure. Feelings of pleasure and disappointment are part of the feedback mechanism that helps your brain decide between productive and useless behaviors. Rewards close the feedback loop and finish the habit cycle.

Personal Finance: Continuous Learning and Growth

Continuous learning is vital to gaining financial independence, yet many people frequently overlook it. Learning and adapting to changes in the financial market, economy, and technology is critical for establishing a stable financial future. Learning can take many forms, including self-education, official education, and mentoring. Here, we'll look at some advantages of continual learning for obtaining financial independence and how it might affect your financial path.

Continuous learning enhances financial literacy. Financial literacy refers to the capacity to comprehend and manage your finances properly. It is critical for making sound financial decisions, such as investing, budgeting, and saving. Continuous learning can help you develop financial literacy by teaching you concepts like compound interest, diversification, and risk management. Aside from the information in this book, additional ways to gain financial literacy include attending seminars, reading financial books like this one, and taking online courses.

Continuous learning allows you to stay current with market trends and technology advancements: The market and technology are always evolving, and keeping up with these developments is critical to financial freedom. Continuous learning lets you stay up to speed on market trends such as interest rate changes, stock market performance, and economic data. Furthermore, technology is rapidly changing how we handle our finances, and continuous learning allows you to adopt new technologies to help you manage your finances more efficiently. Budgeting apps, investing platforms, and digital wallets are some examples of financial management tools.

Continuous learning improves your career possibilities. Continuous learning can help you develop your skills and knowledge, boosting your long-term employment possibilities. Acquiring new skills and information allows you to be more competitive in the job market and negotiate higher compensation. Furthermore, you could consider beginning a side hustle or a business related to your abilities and hobbies.

Continuous learning helps you make smart investment decisions: As stated, making informed investment selections is critical in obtaining financial independence. Continuous learning lets you learn about many investing alternatives, including stocks, bonds, and real estate. You can also learn about different investment techniques, such as diversification, value, and growth. Furthermore, constant learning can help you comprehend the risks and returns connected with various assets, allowing you to make better investing selections.

Continuous learning is vital for reaching financial independence. You will create a secure financial future by improving your financial literacy, staying current on market trends and technological improvements, expanding your employment opportunities, and making smart investment decisions. It's never too late to start studying, and numerous resources are accessible, including books, classes, and mentorship programs.

www.ingramcontent.com/pod-product-compliance
Lightning Source LLC
Chambersburg PA
CBHW071827210526
45479CB00001B/27